THE LACE CURTAINS OF BERLIN

Though oblivious to most people, the lace curtains send out messages. At first glance they seem ugly, tacky, sometimes even barbaric, the textile equivalent to sauerkraut with bratwurst. But eventually you learn to love them. Because tackiness, when taken to extremes, can acquire a poetic dimension.

The purpose of this lace-curtain fashion show is to delight the eye and intrigue the mind. The 196 pictures in this collection are in reality proxy portraits of Berliners and their lifestyles. To those who will make it to Berlin, it's an appetizer. To the majority who won't, it's the only chance to experience this wonderful example of textile poetry.

THE LACE CURTAINS OF BERLIN

IZAI AMORIM

First edition: 2013
Published by Izai Amorim

ISBN Numbers:
978-1494320263 — Softcover (Amazon distribution)
978-3982165691 — Softcover (Ingram distribution)

Photographs, text, and book design by Izai Amorim

Author's website: www.izaiamorim.com

Book website: www.lacecurtains.izaiamorim.com

Author's mailing list: www.mailinglist.izaiamorim.com

Contents

In memory of
Rainer-Werner Sprengberg

Twin Projects: Berlin

"The Lace Curtains of Berlin" is the graphic, non-fiction part of the "Twin Projects: Berlin." The fiction part is the novel "The Games." There is a character in the novel called Rainer-Werner Sprengberg who photographs lace curtains. These are "his" curtains.

You can find lace curtains anywhere in Berlin. I chose to photograph them in the neighborhoods of Kreuzberg and Neukölln. It took me a whole summer to finish the project. I had to shoot on the weekends, and I needed good weather.

You can photograph the lace curtains for only two to three hours in the early morning, because once the sun gets to a certain height, the windows reflect light like mirrors. You have to hit the road at about 6 a.m. and keep walking, searching, and shooting. For this reason, I don't know where and when each photograph was shot. There was no time for recordkeeping.

I shot more than a thousand black-and-white pictures. Here I show only a fraction, 196 pictures. Shooting the pictures was the easy part. The challenge was choosing which curtains to show, and in which order. After innumerable trials I decided to group them according to window type.

I identified eight different families, or collections, of windows. I named them after streets in the Görlitzer Park area of the Kreuzberg neighborhood, an area I am very fond of. This doesn't mean that all the lace curtains in a given collection were photographed on the street the collection is named after. As I said above, I can't say where each picture was shot.

Archaeological Experiment

There are a lot of ways to learn about a given group of people. One can ask them about their worldview, their hopes and dreams, their history. One can observe how they live, talk, eat, dress, work, have fun. One can investigate what kinds of things they have.

Things are a very powerful reservoir of information. But since language is a much more effective medium of communication, we tend to pay attention to words and to ignore objects. With time, we even lose the ability to understand the messages they send. We could learn a lot from archaeologists. Though they normally have only a few remaining things belonging to an extinct group of people, they can still tell us a lot about this group.

The project "The Lace Curtains of Berlin" is a kind of archaeological experiment. Unlike true archaeology, it does not deal with an extinct group of people, but with an existing one. It doesn't look under the earth, but behind windows. It doesn't use shovels and brushes, but a camera. Like archaeology, it studies things used by a certain group of people in order to investigate who they are.

The people in question are the Berliners, and the things studied are their lace curtains. Though oblivious to most people, the curtains send out messages and tell almost as much about the people behind them as any anthropological study would.

The lace curtains shown in this book are only a very small sample of what is available. There are literally hundreds of different kinds. To those readers who will make it to Berlin, it's an appetizer. To the majority who won't, it's the only chance to experience this wonderful example of textile poetry.

The aesthetic experience is complemented by the intellectual challenge of trying to understand the people behind the curtains. The curtain ensemble possesses a puzzle-like dimension. Single puzzle pieces don't tell much individually, and only start making sense when put together. The more puzzle pieces you have, the better you can recognize the picture.

The purpose of this archaeological experiment is to delight the eye and to intrigue the mind, to show the curtains and let them send their messages. The reader is invited to enjoy the lace curtains' textile poetry and to decipher the puzzle.

Poetic Dimension

This is a very subjective essay. It's unorthodox, unscientific, literary. It's based on observation, not scholarship. It's about perceptions, which could as well be misperceptions. It connects things that shouldn't necessarily be connected, and makes conclusions that could be false. It definitely makes generalizations, which are never true.

* * *

Once, back in the golden twenties of the last century, Berlin was a great city to live in — cosmopolitan, vibrant, exciting, avant-garde. Then came the thirties with the brown shirts, followed by the forties, with destruction and death. Berlin was never to recover its glamour.

The sixties brought the wall, transforming this city into something unique. Some things cannot be described, they have to be experienced: to live on a capitalist island right in the middle of a communist country, surrounded by a wall; to know that, if the third world war ever happened, it would start here. To live a normal life despite all that — that was what Berlin became.

The nineties brought reconstruction, fueled by the desire to make Berlin a normal city again. It cleaned it up and made it nice and tidy, along the way robbing Berlin of its last charms: its past, its history, its scars, its ruins, its decadence.

The reconstruction is practically finished, and almost all these goals have been achieved. Berlin has become just like any other German city.

There's not much to say about Berlin's new architecture, the so-called historical reconstruction. The fear of diversity, the irrational urge to control chaos, the aversion to experiments, the lack of vision, and last but not least, the nostalgic flight back to an idealized past — all this has left its mark. There are a few exceptions, but one needs only two words to categorize these new, uninspiring, well-behaved, boring, look-alike buildings: rearranging rectangles. One day people will look back at this missed opportunity with regret.

But forget the boring architecture. If for any reason you happen to find yourself in Berlin, there's something much better to check out. Don't look at the facades, but at what's hanging behind the windows: you will be awed by the lace curtains.

At first glance, the curtains do not look beautiful. They seem ugly, tacky, sometimes even barbaric, the textile equivalent to sauerkraut with bratwurst. You need time to educate your eye and learn to differentiate between them, to enjoy the variations on the same theme, to rejoice when you discover a new type. They are so tacky that sometimes you will laugh out loud, while at other times you will want to cry out even louder.

Slowly your feelings toward the curtains will change. And here comes the scariest part: someday you will lose all your inhibitions and start to love them. Because they transcend their tackiness. The lace curtains of Berlin are the proof that tackiness, when taken to extremes, can acquire a poetic dimension.

RATIBOR STREET COLLECTION

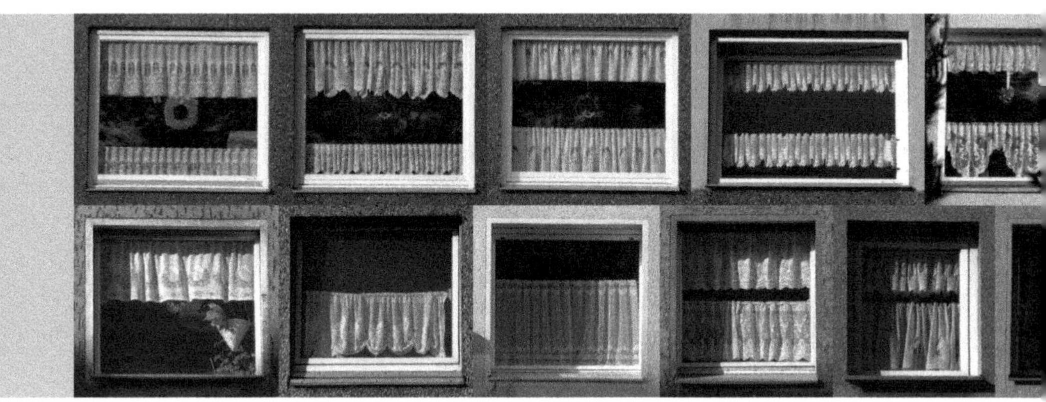

36 pictures

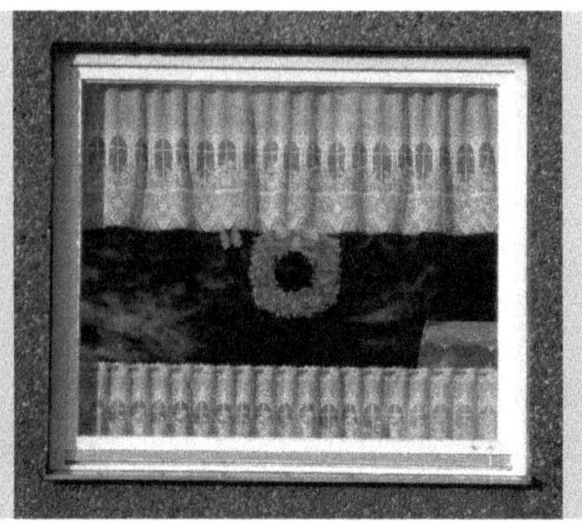

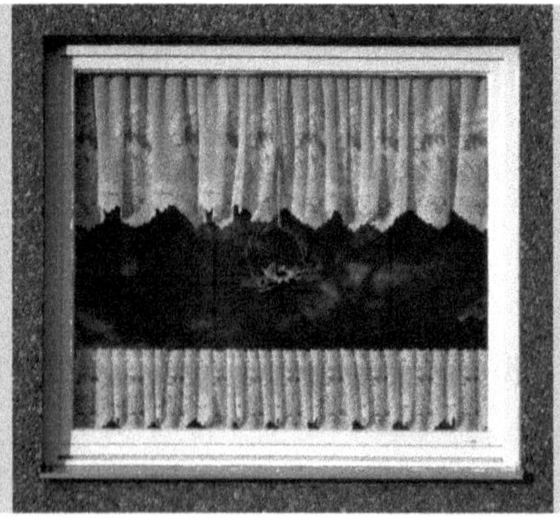

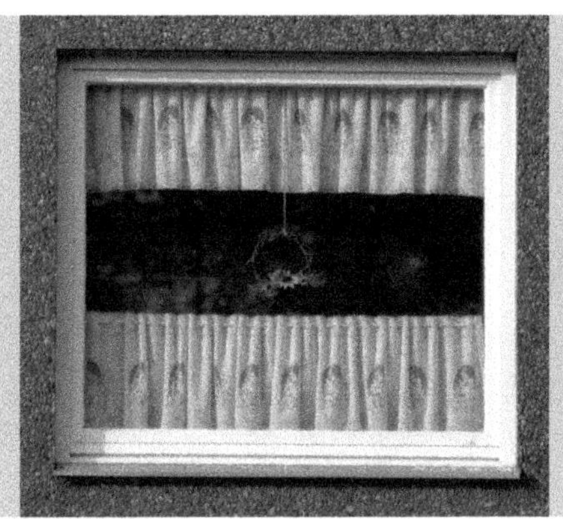

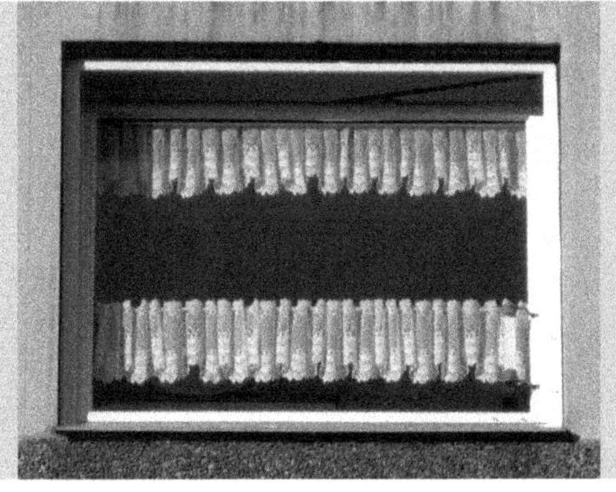

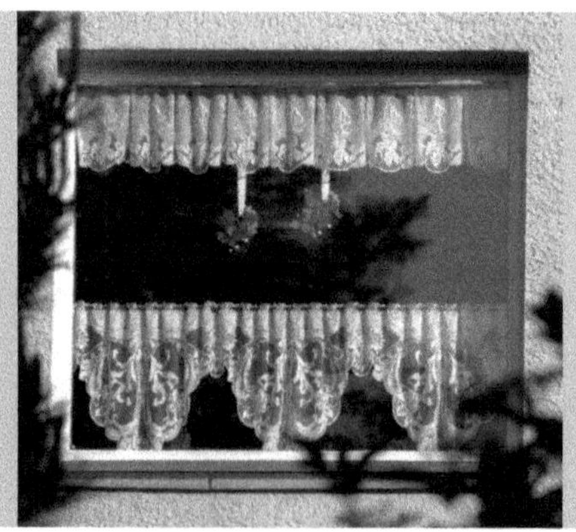

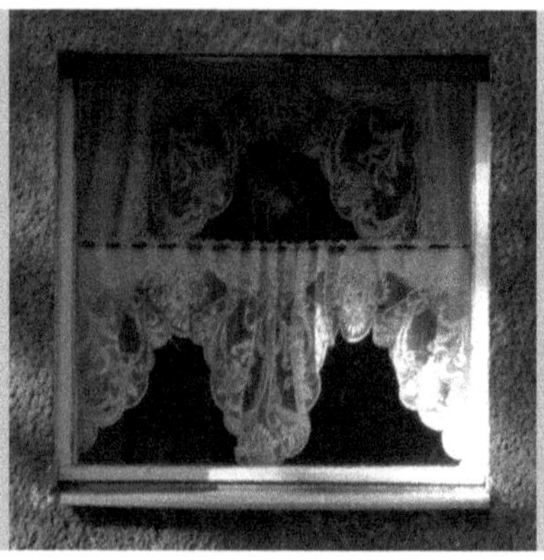

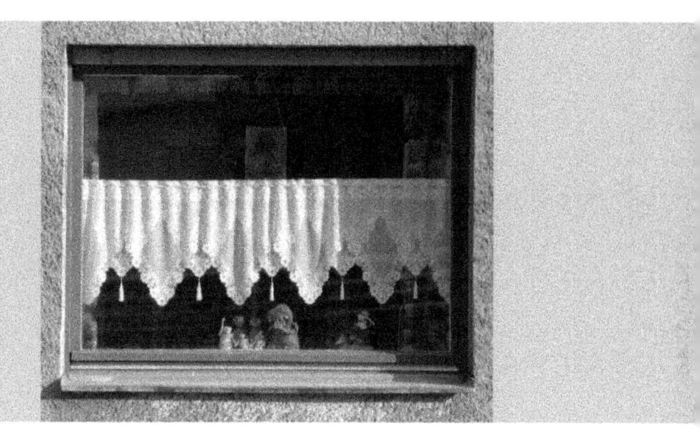

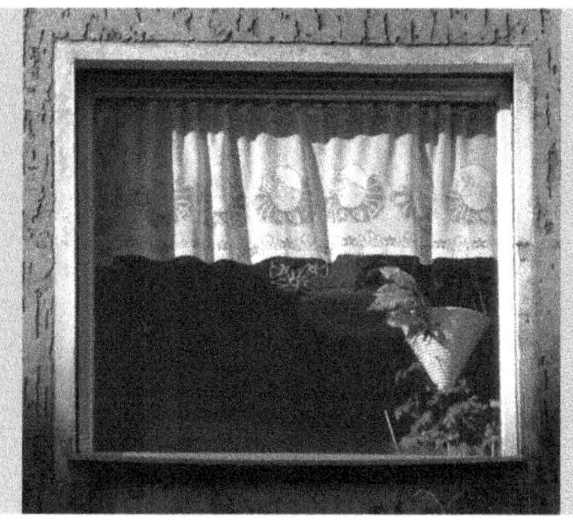

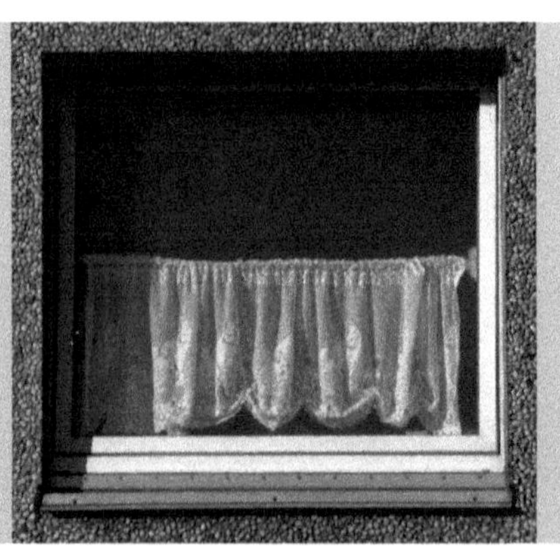

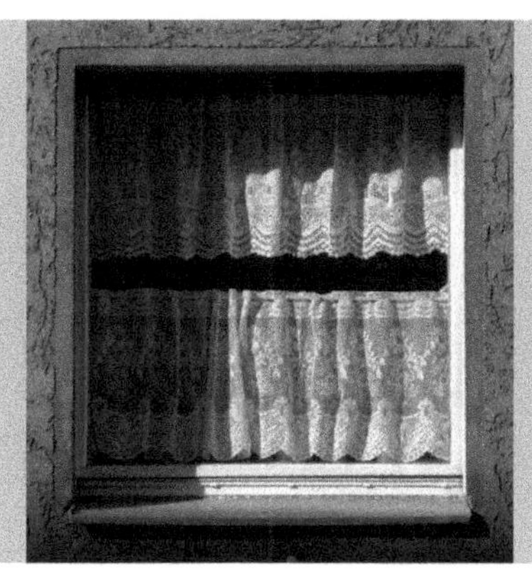

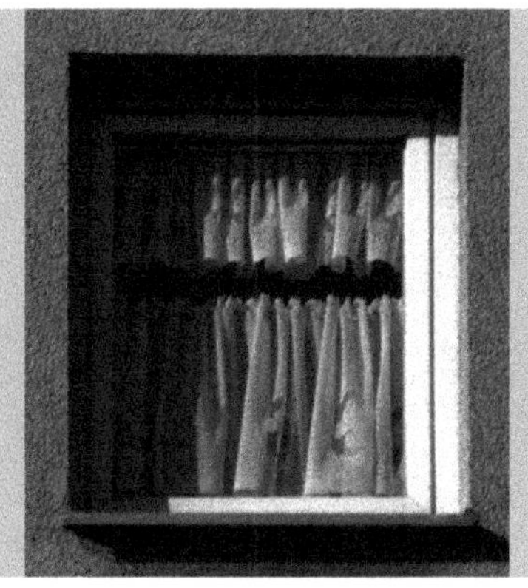

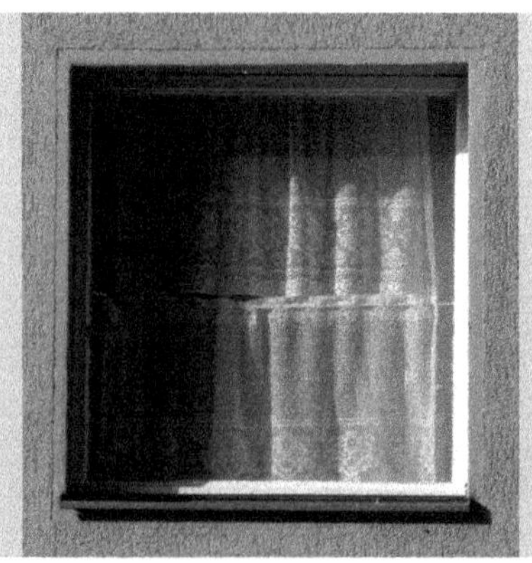

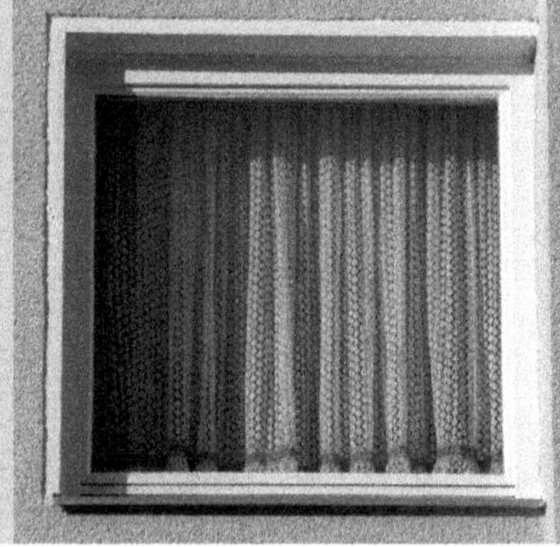

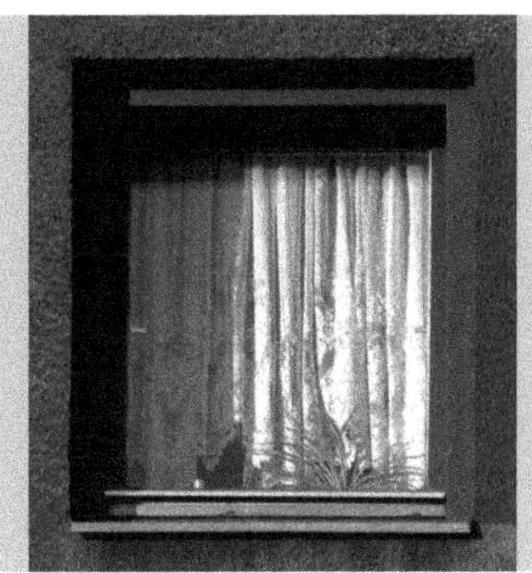

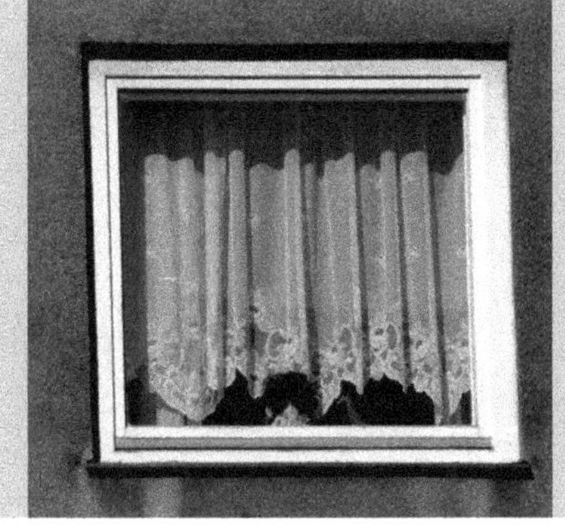

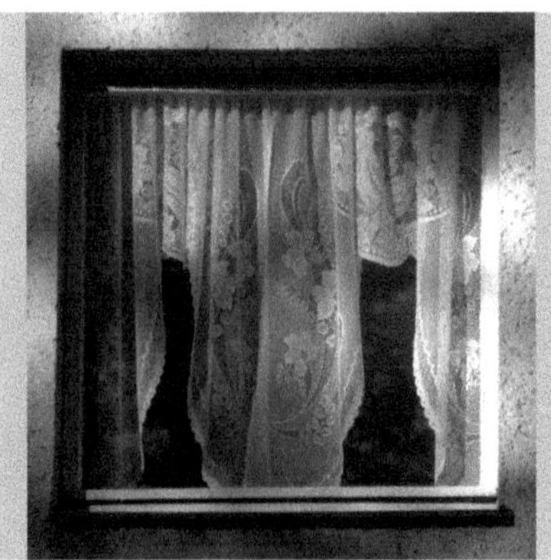

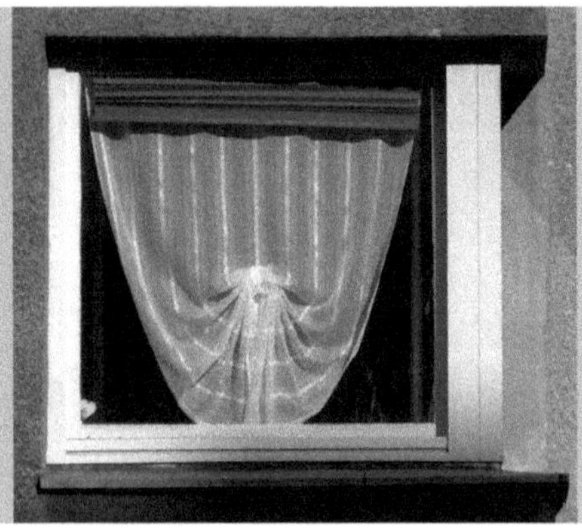

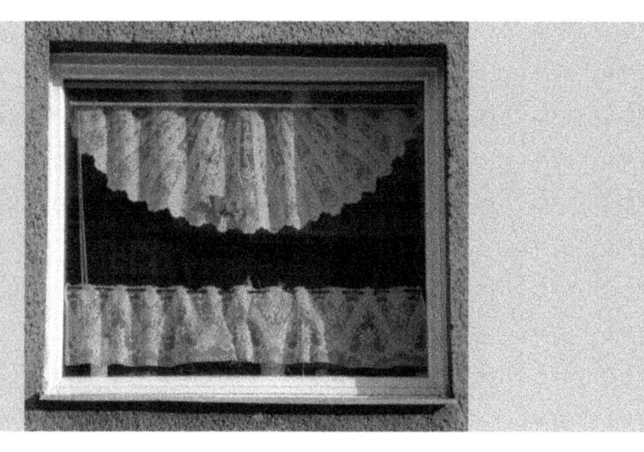

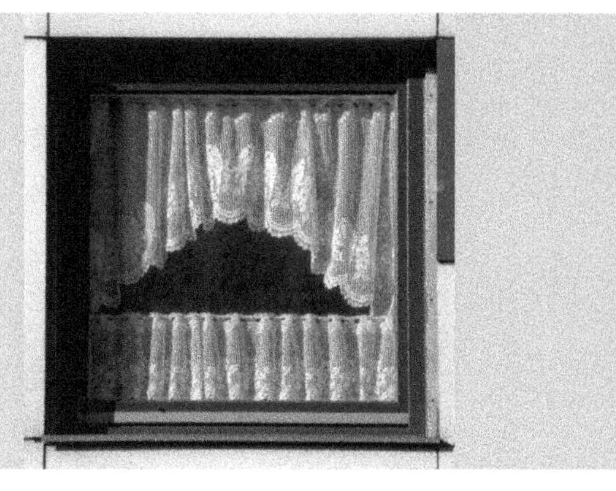

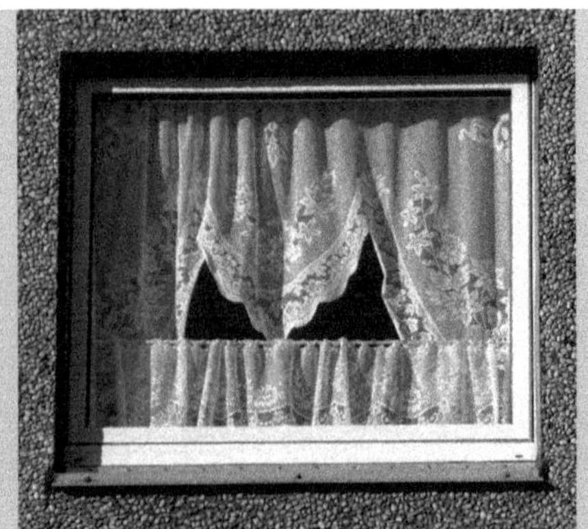

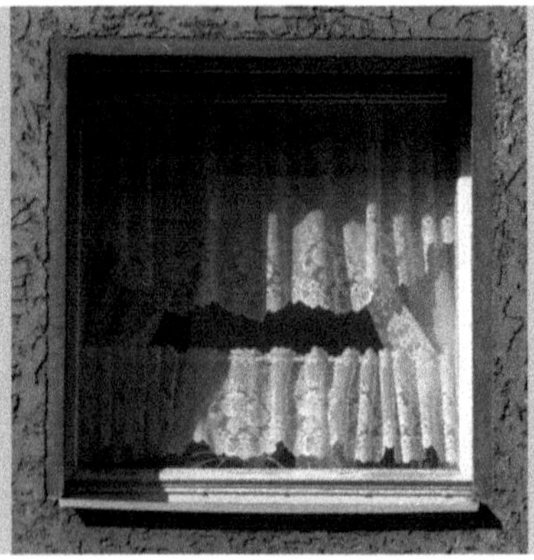

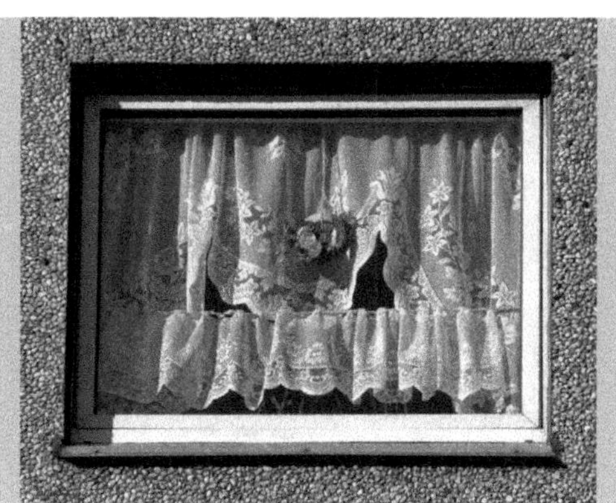

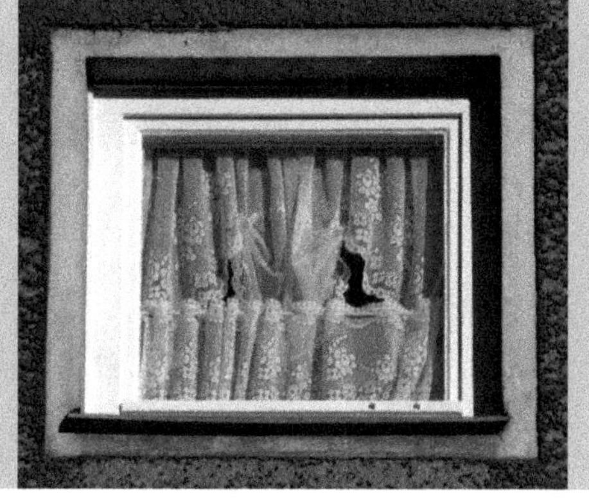

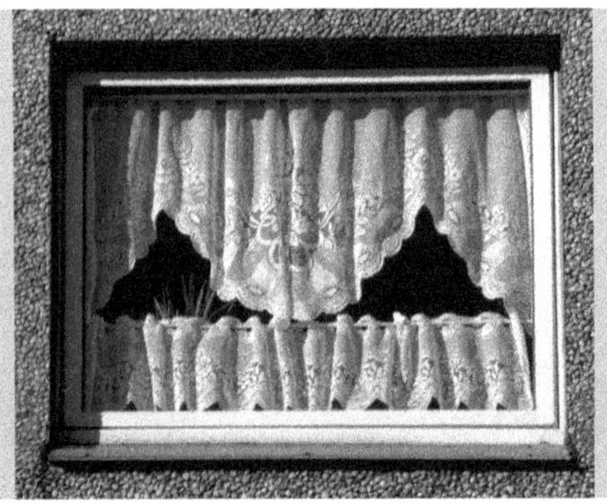

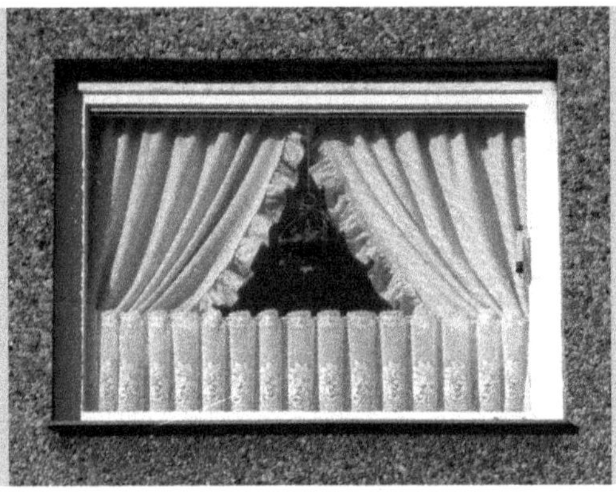

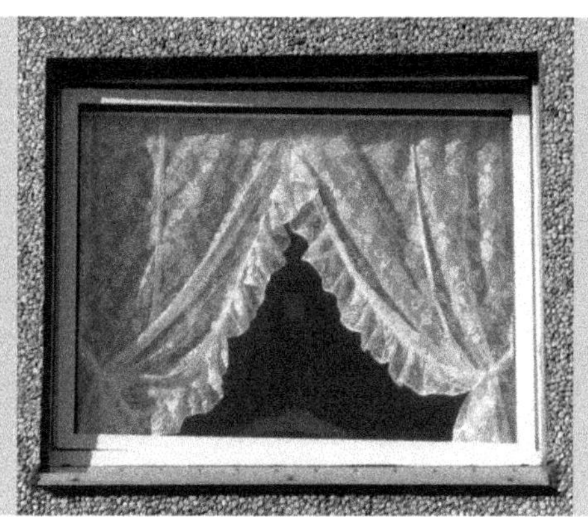

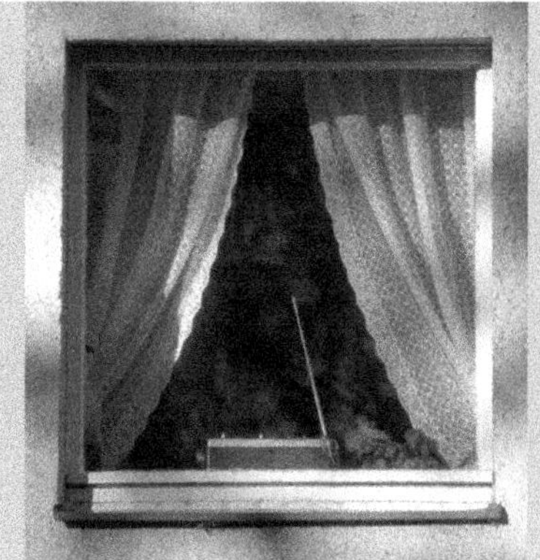

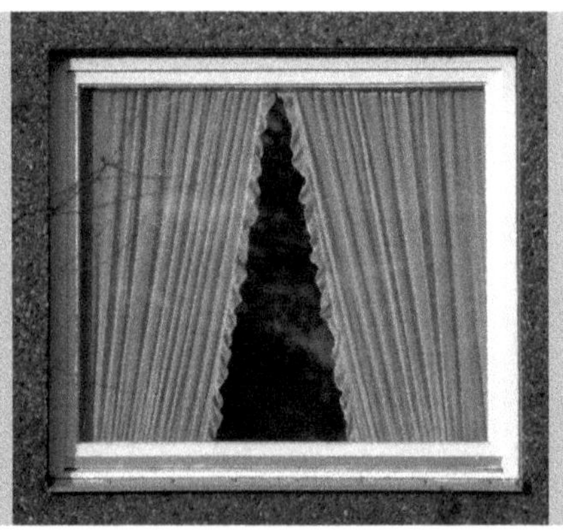

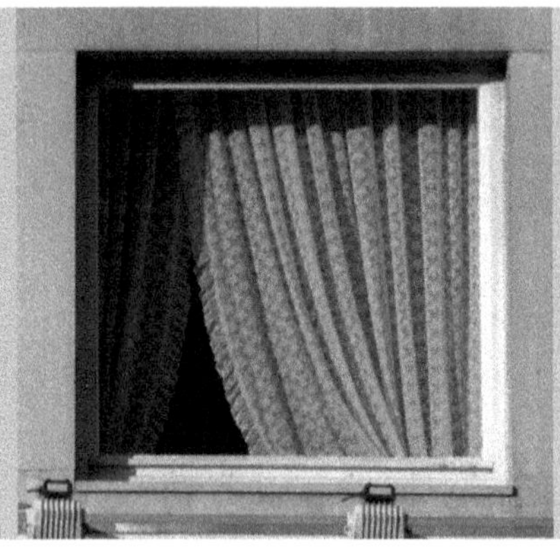

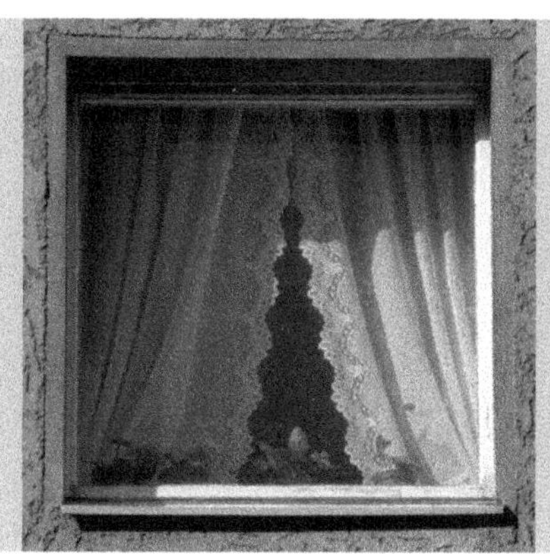

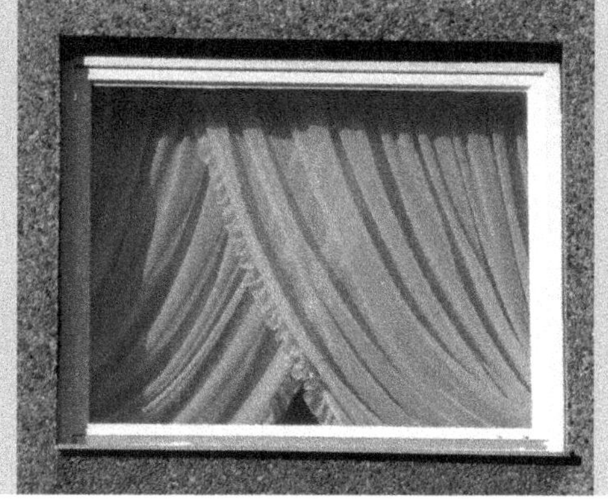

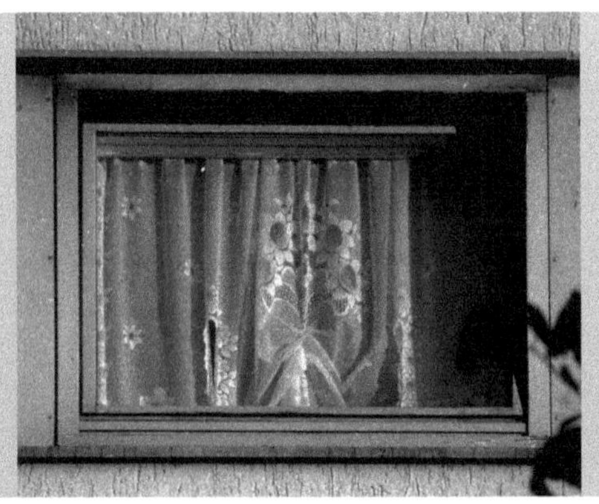

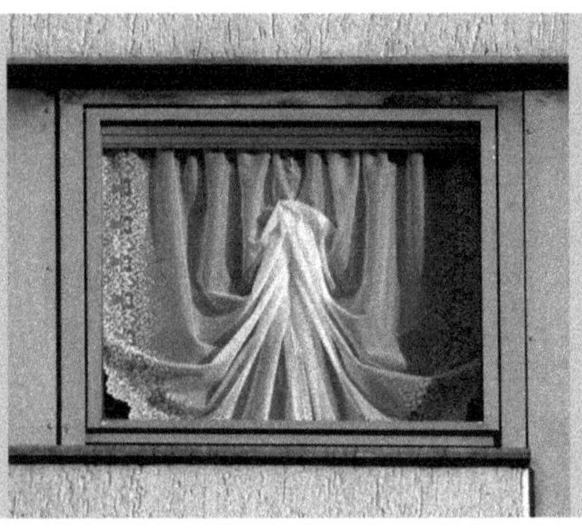

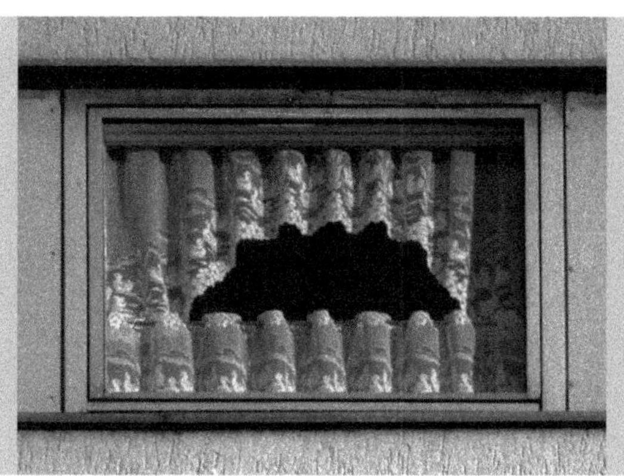

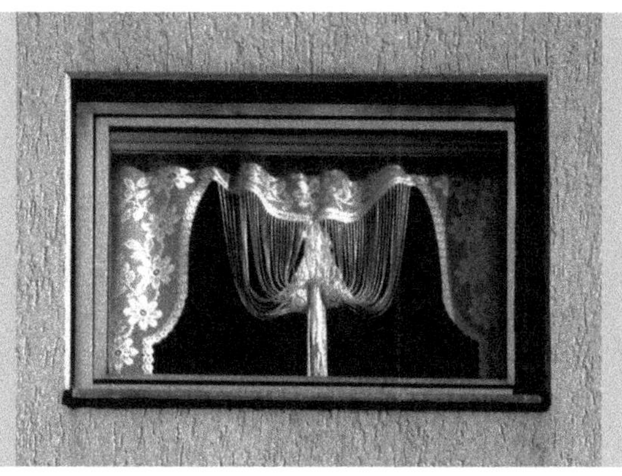

OHLAUER STREET COLLECTION

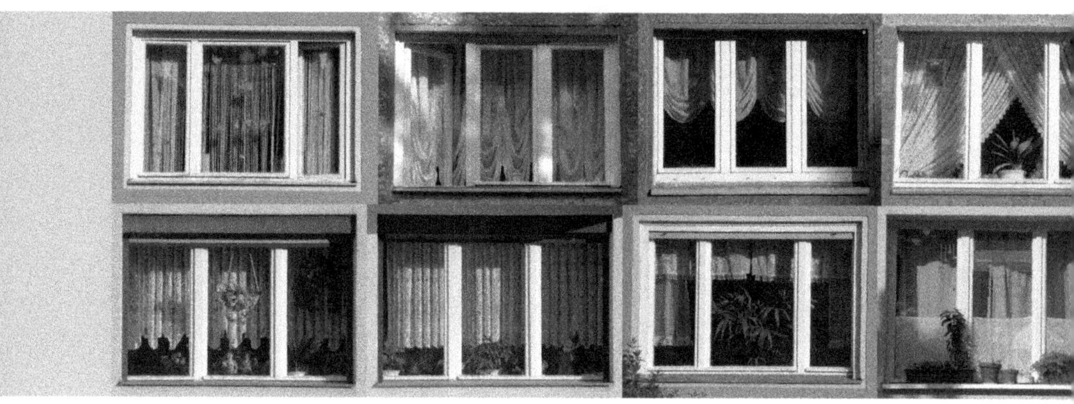

34 pictures

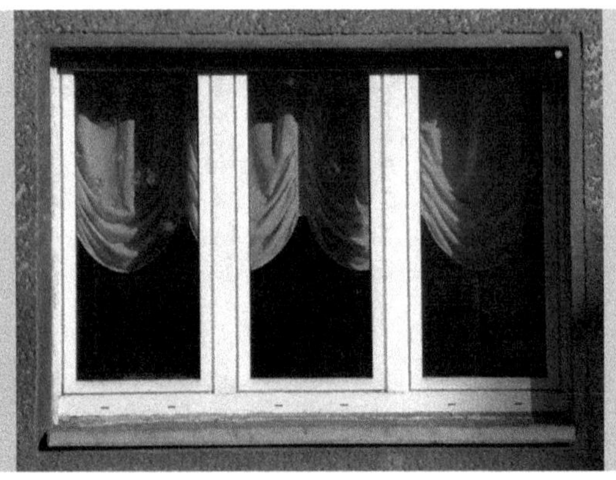

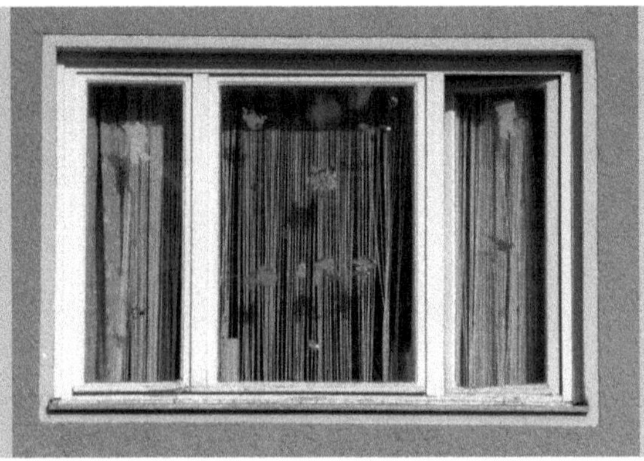

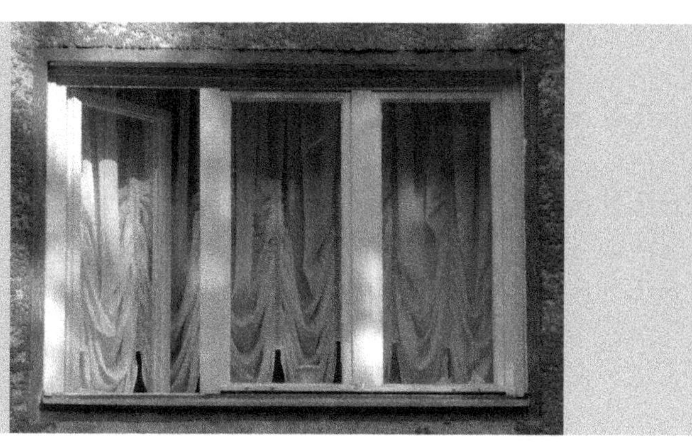

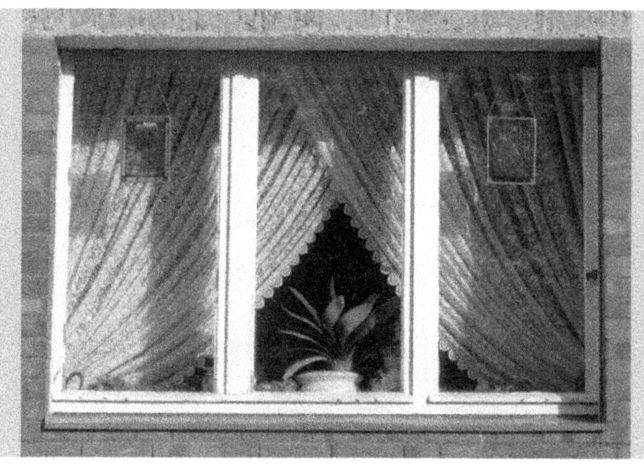

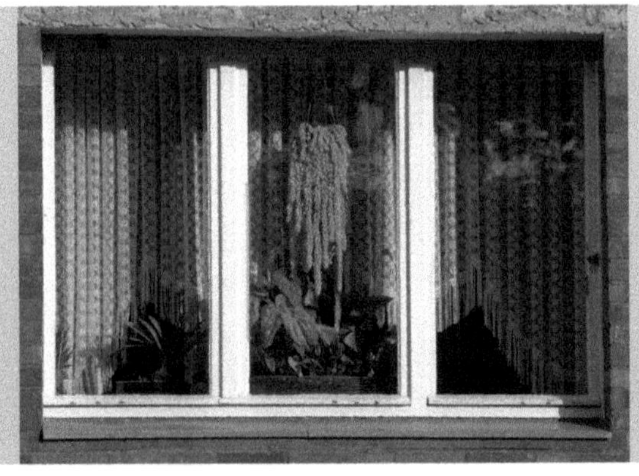

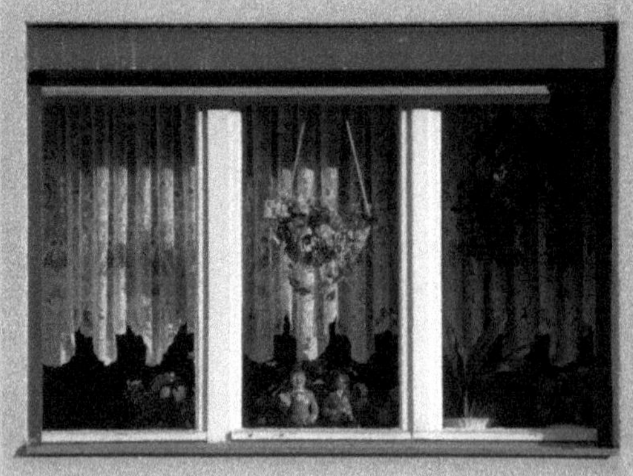

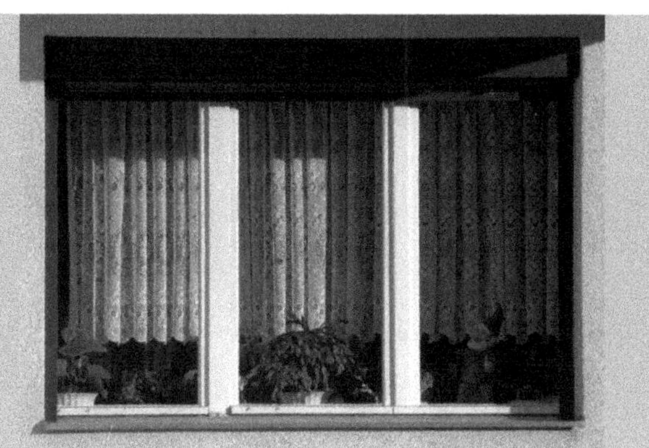

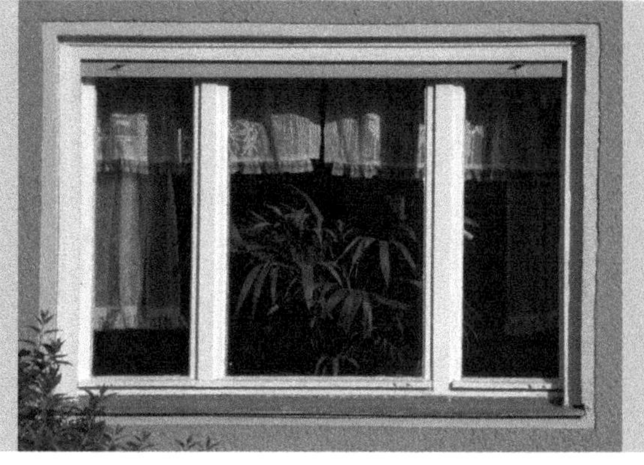

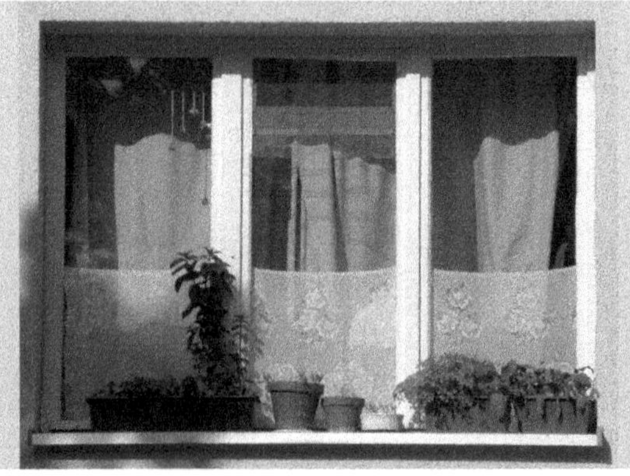

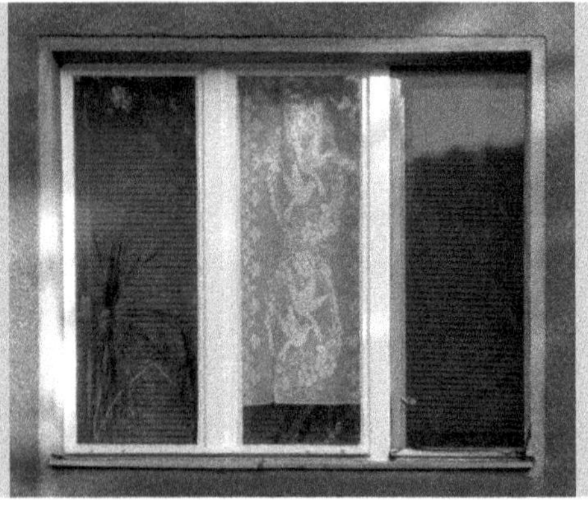

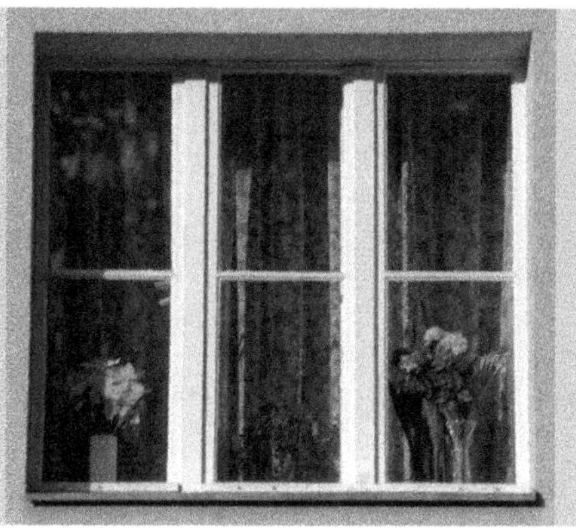

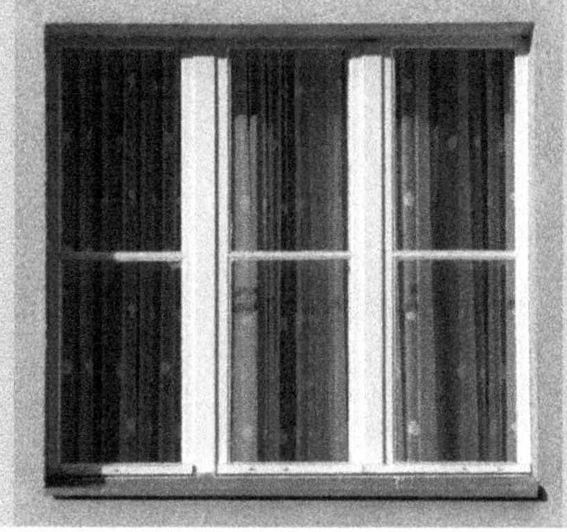

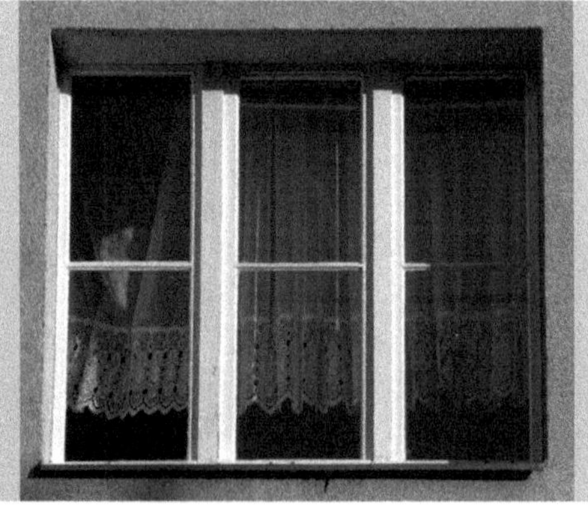

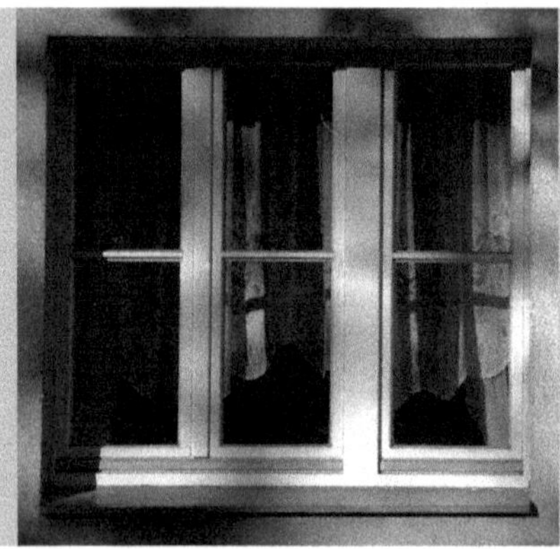

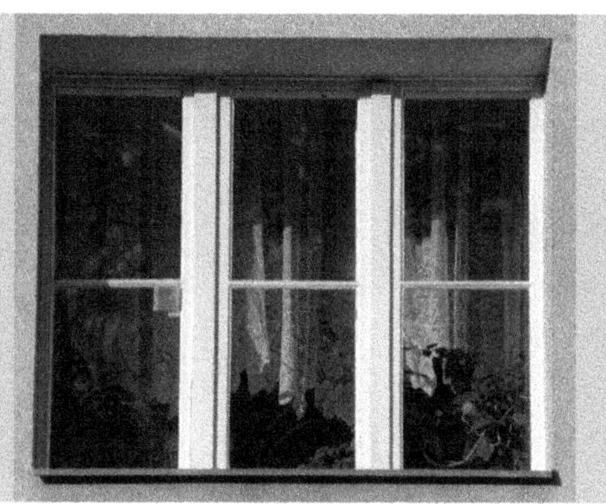

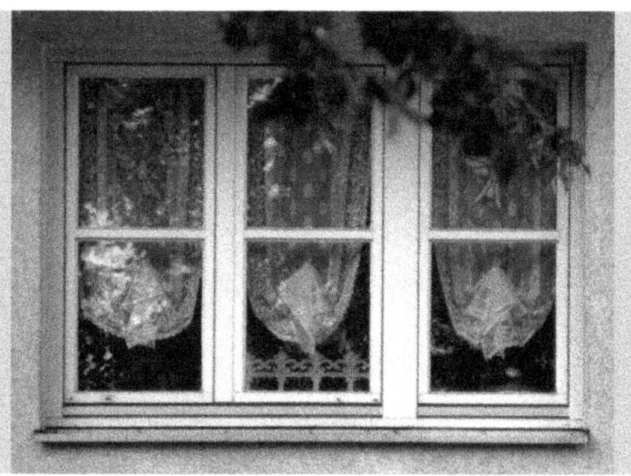

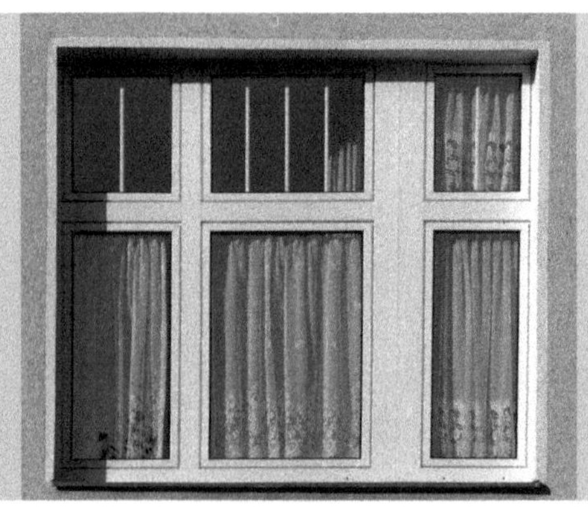

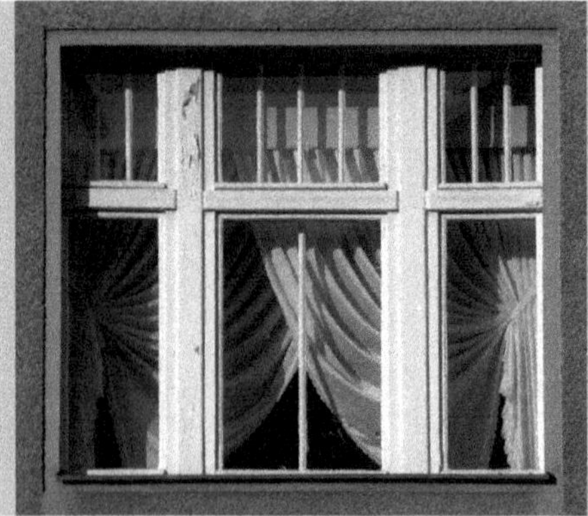

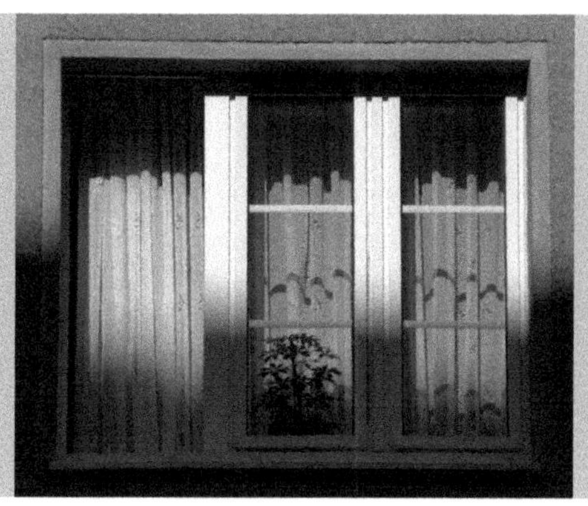

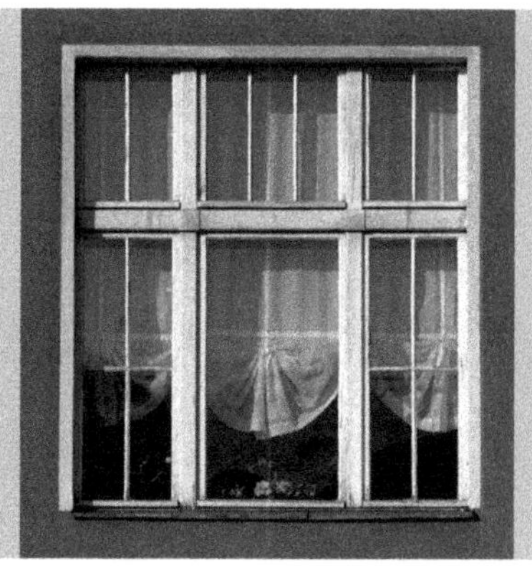

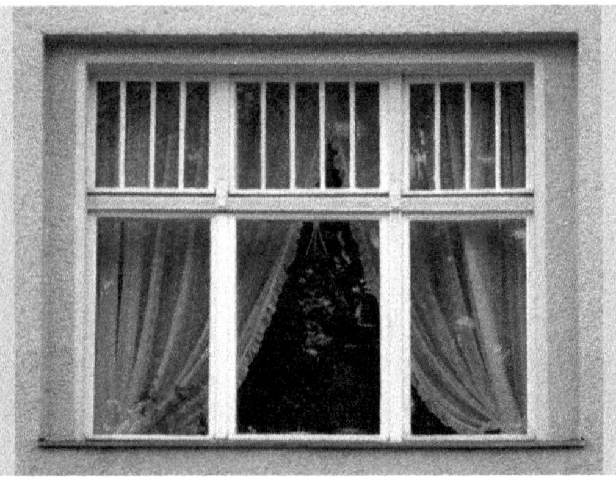

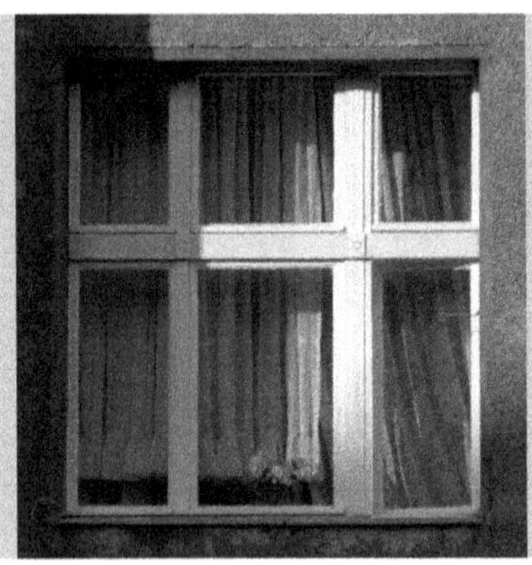

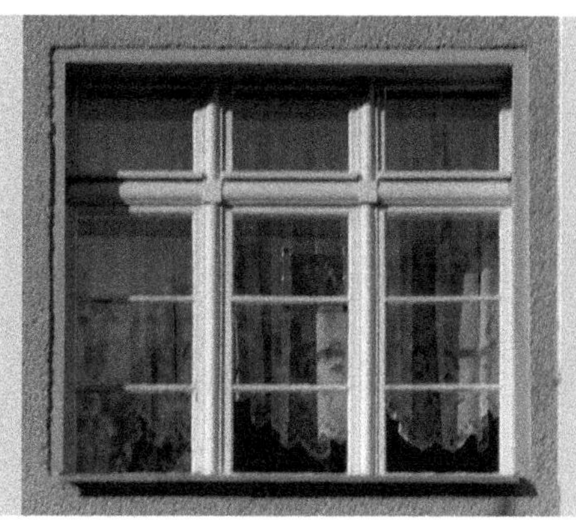

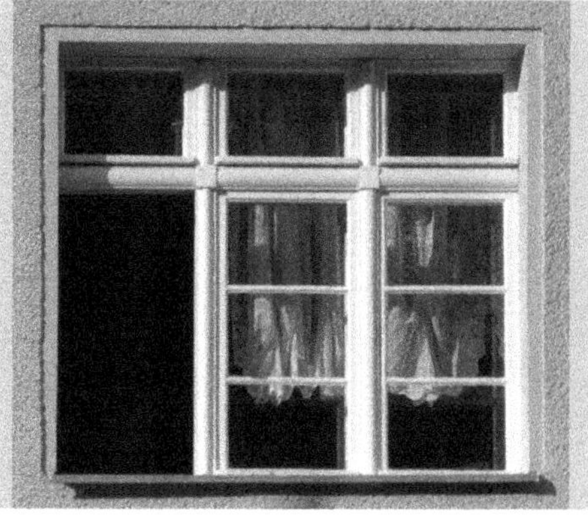

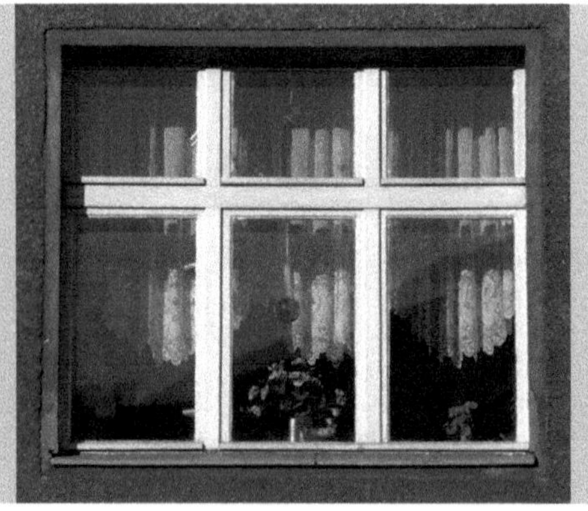

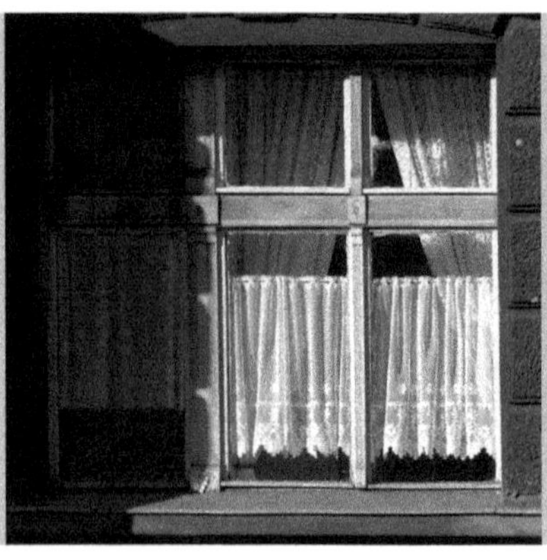

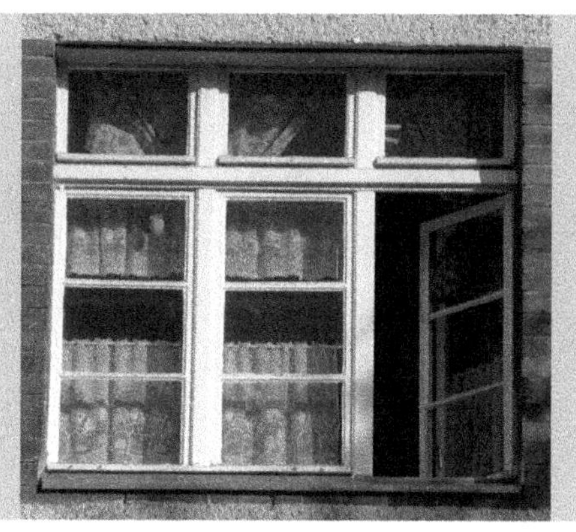

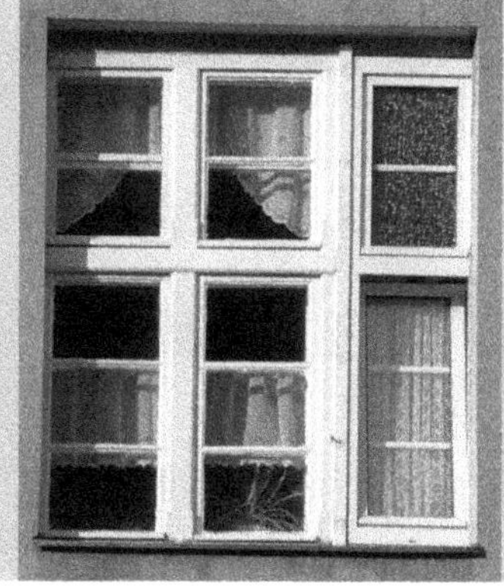

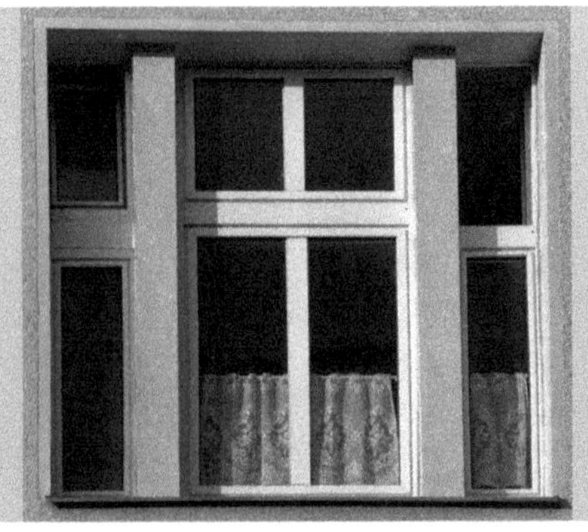

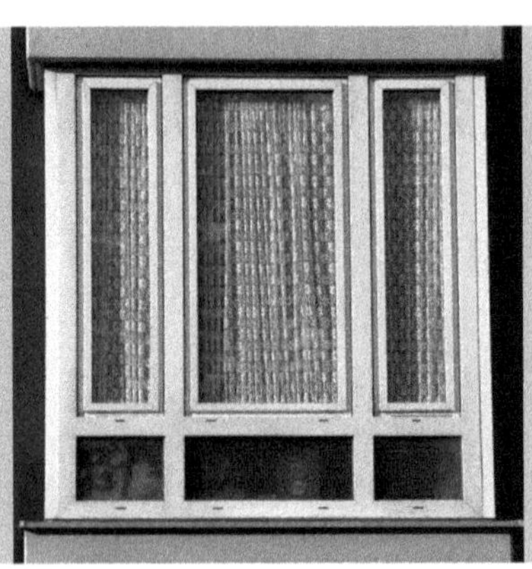

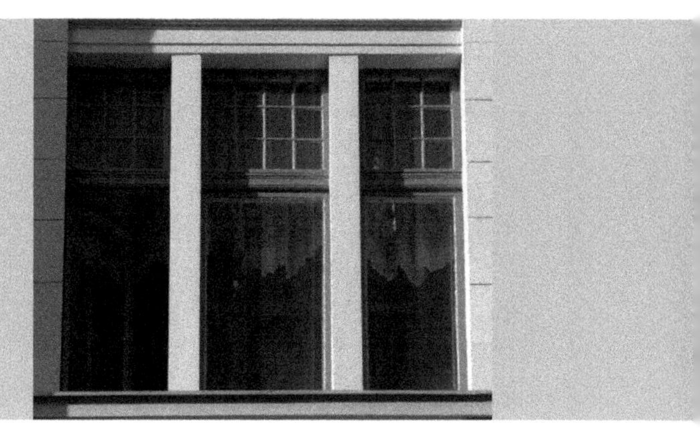

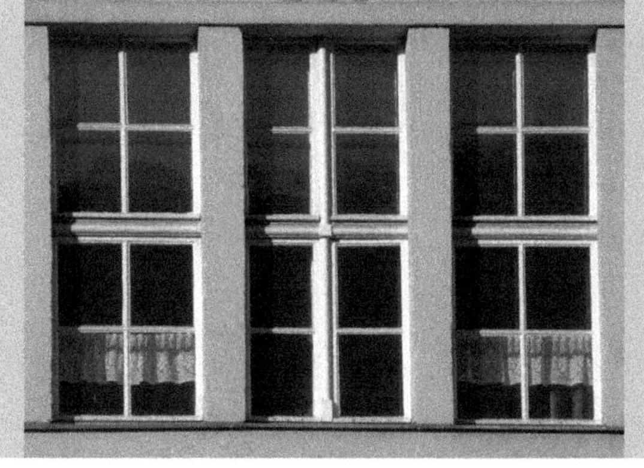

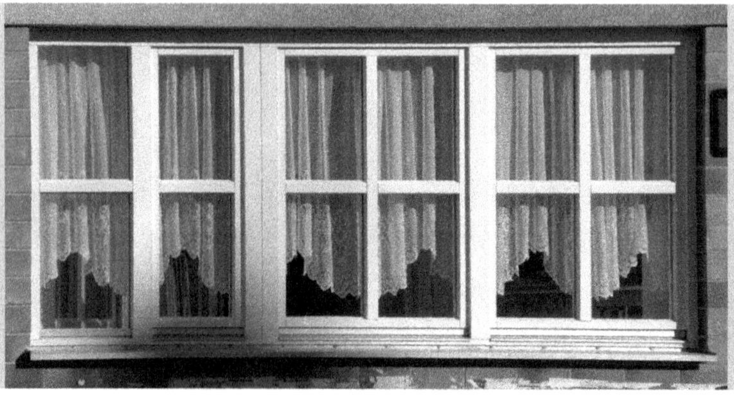

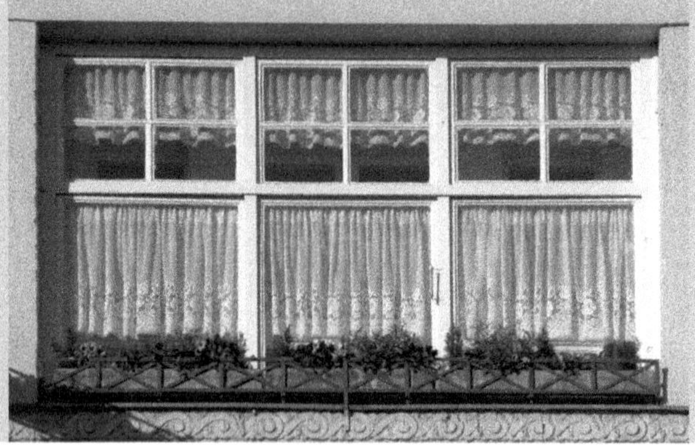

WIENER STREET COLLECTION

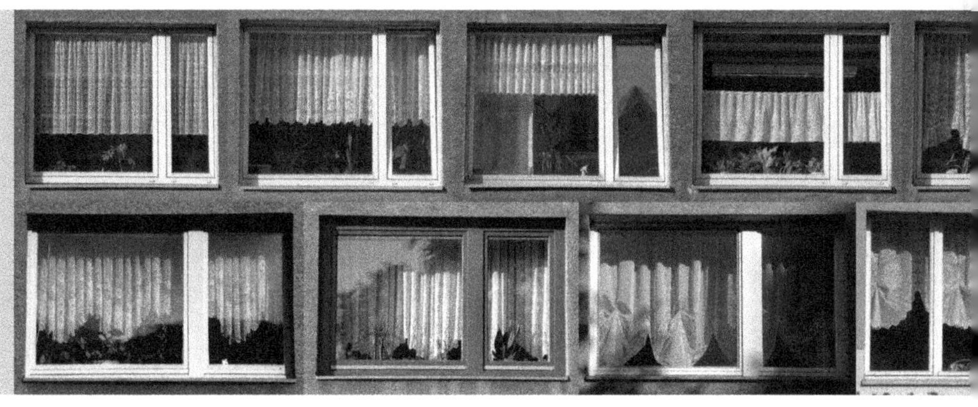

14 pictures

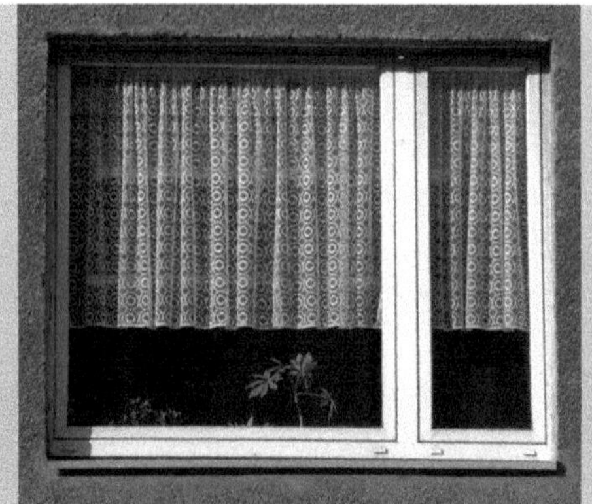

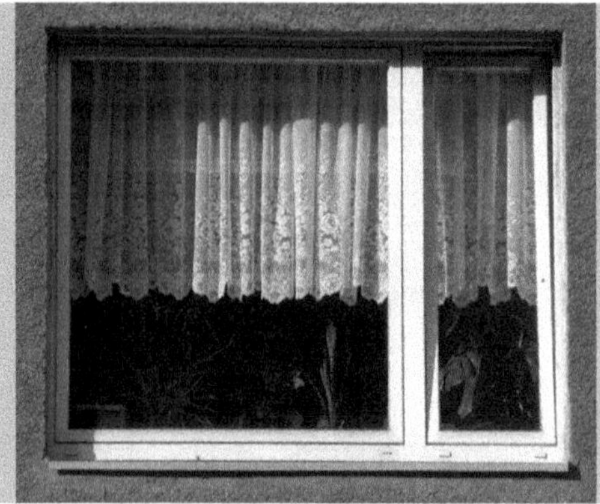

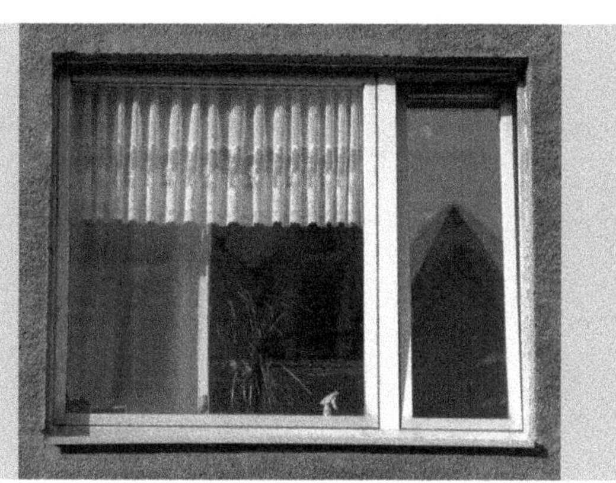

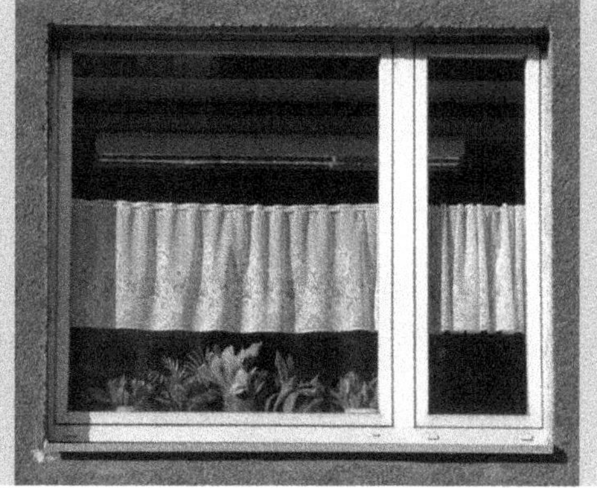

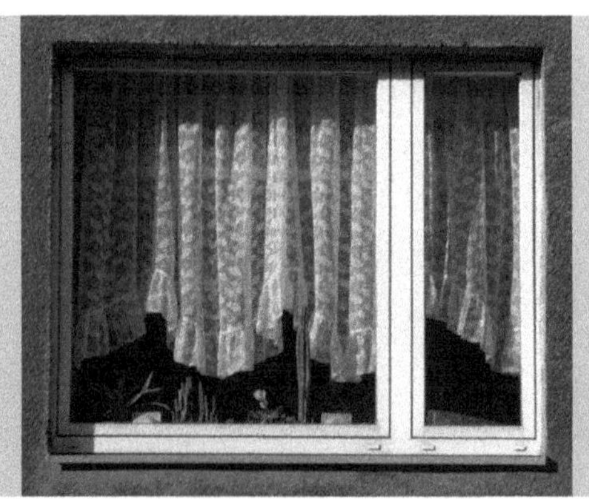

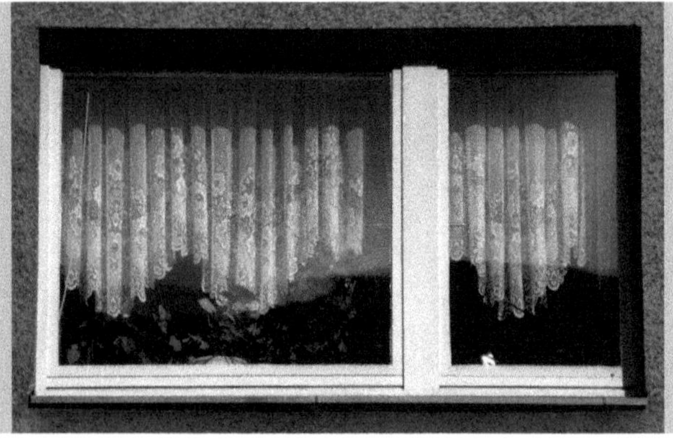

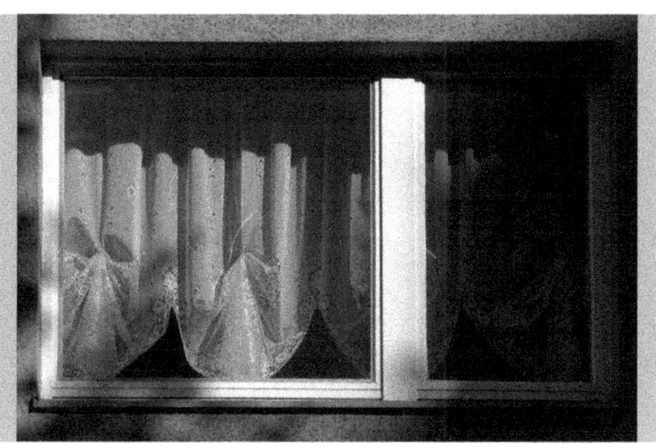

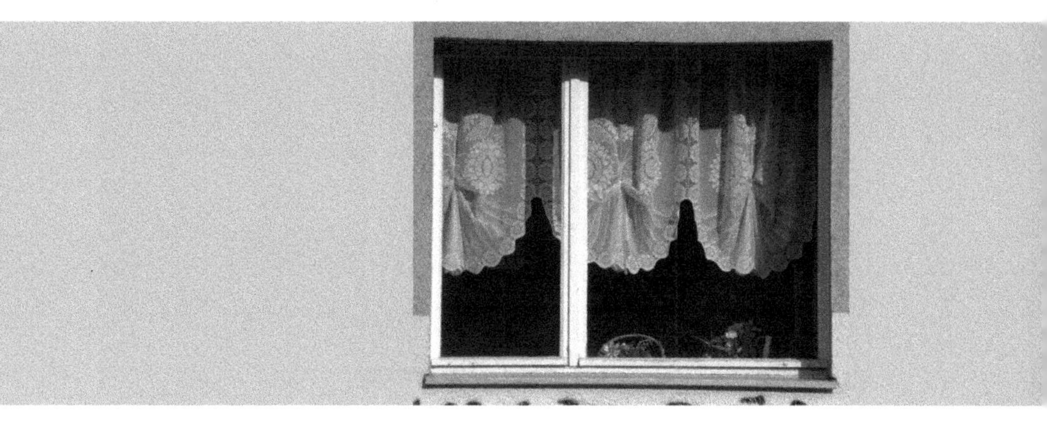

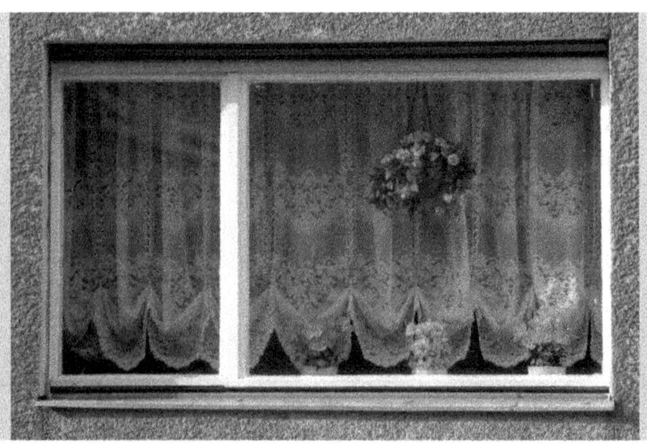

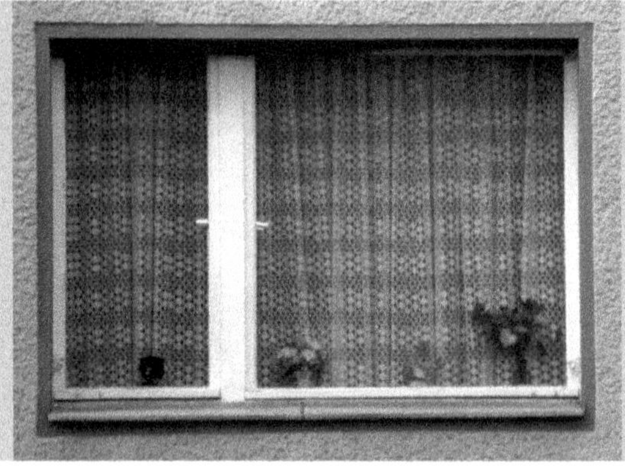

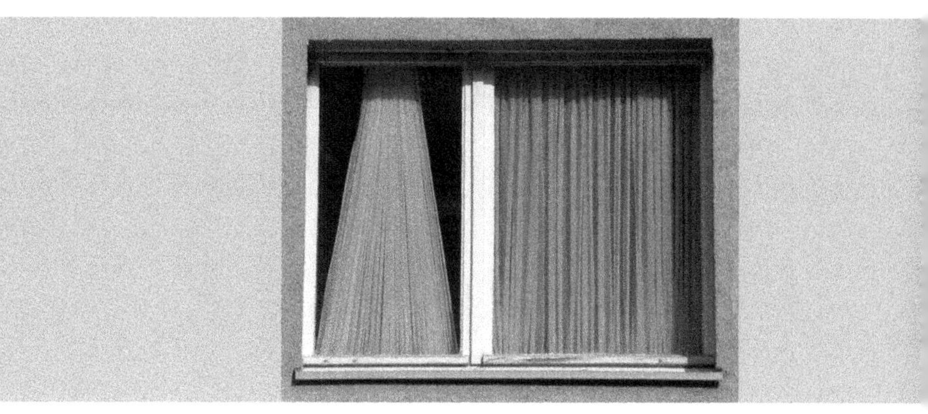

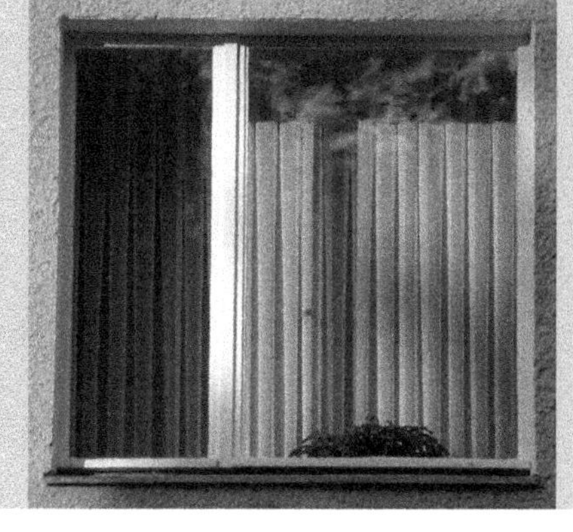

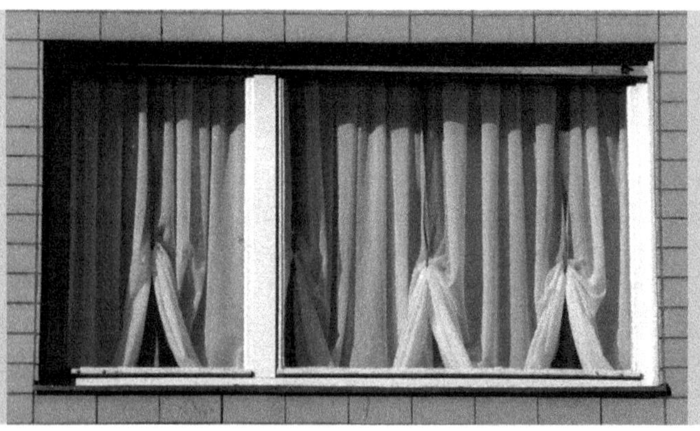

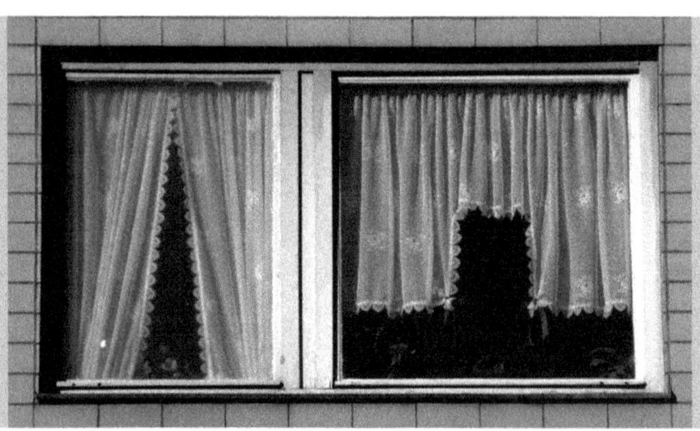

GLOGAUER STREET COLLECTION

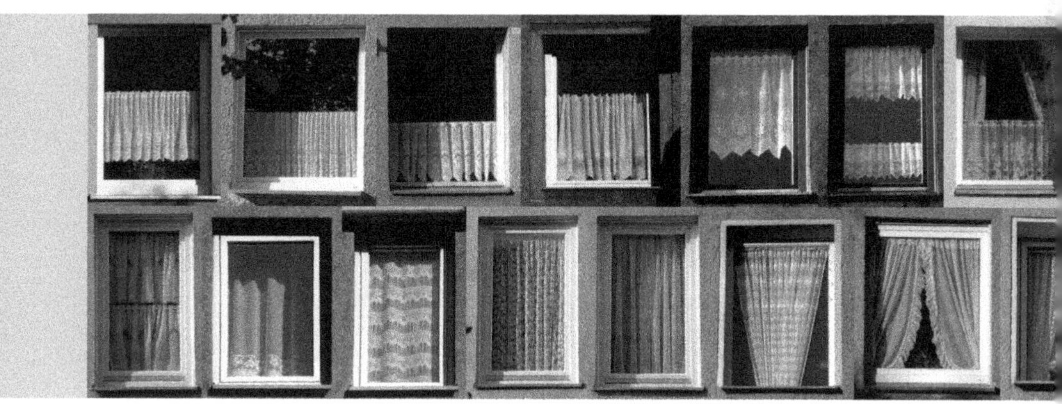

30 pictures

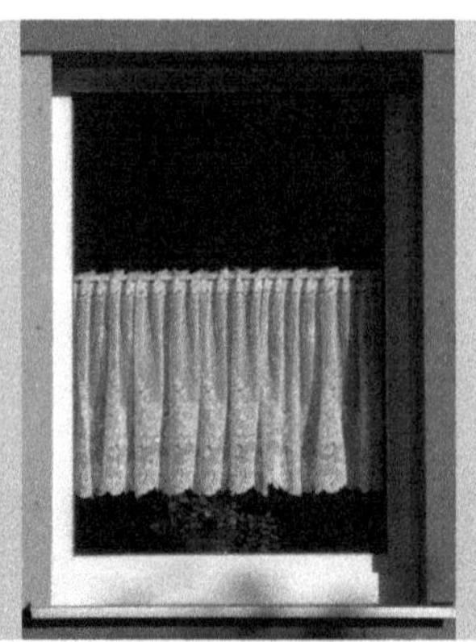

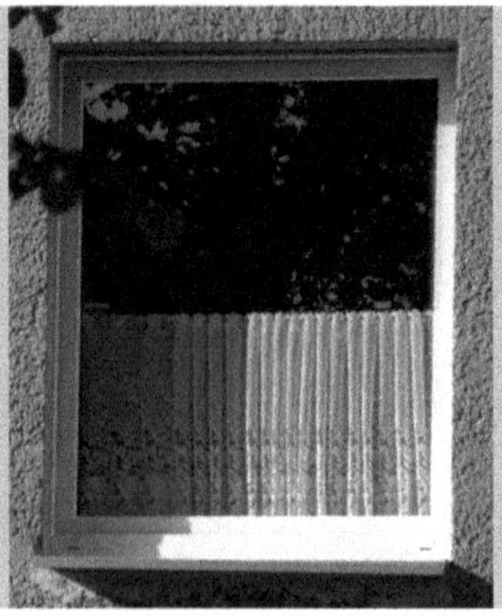

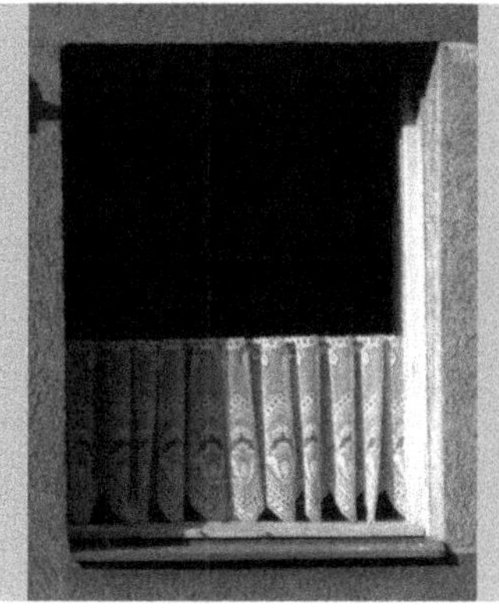

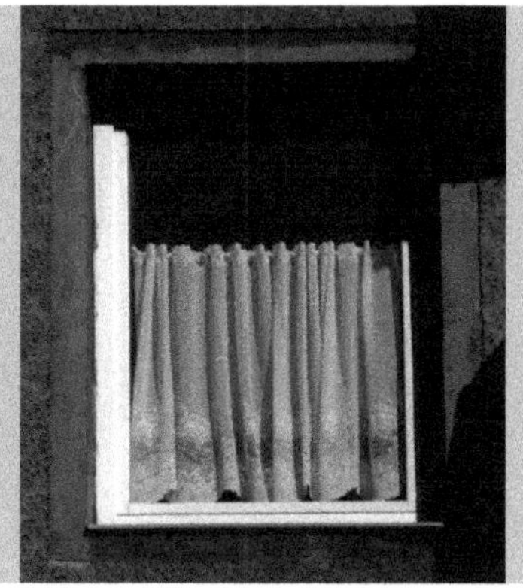

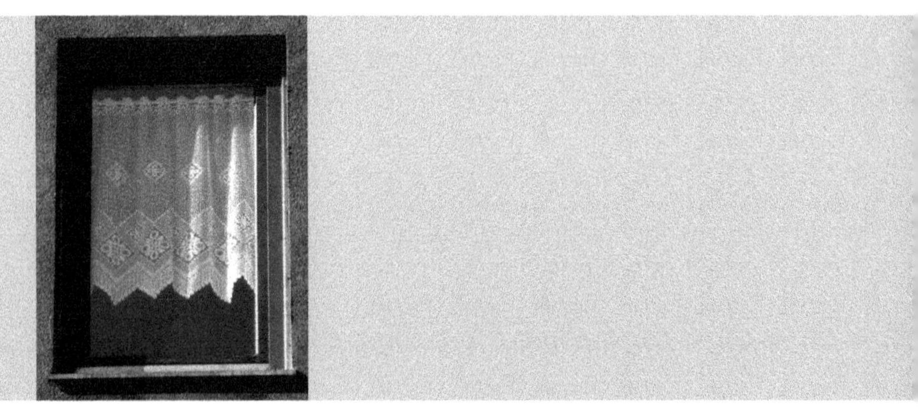

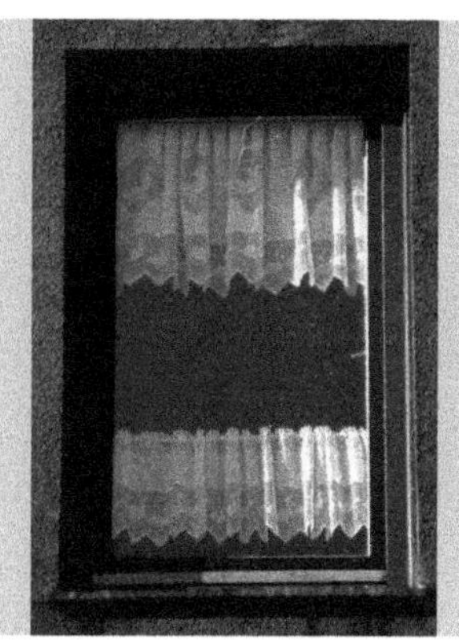

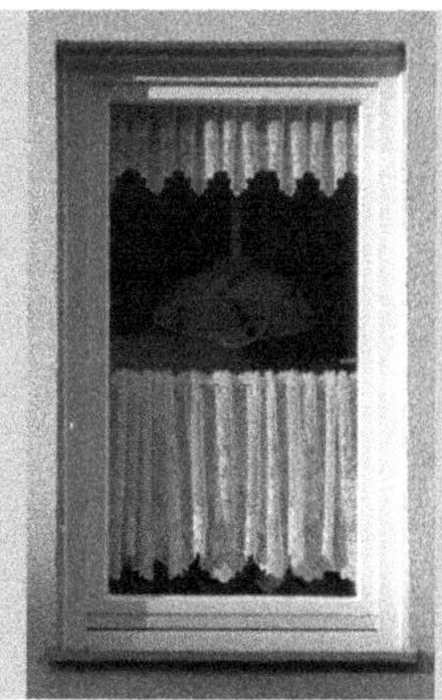

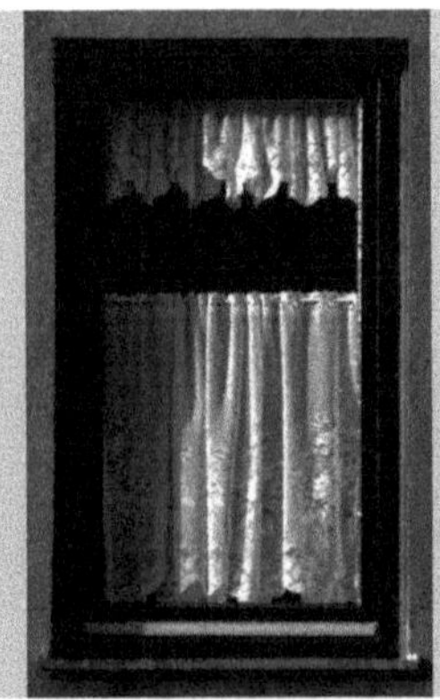

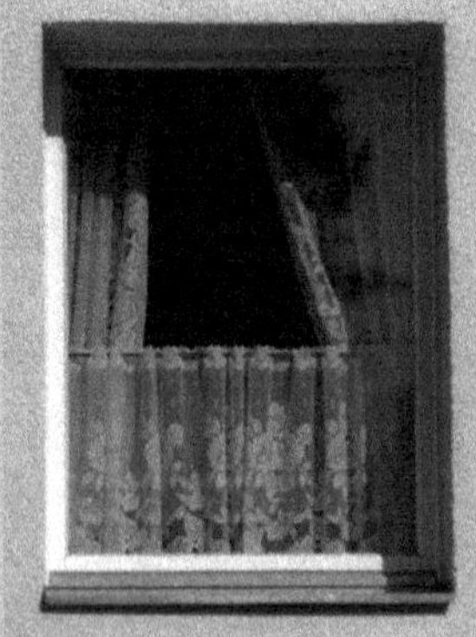

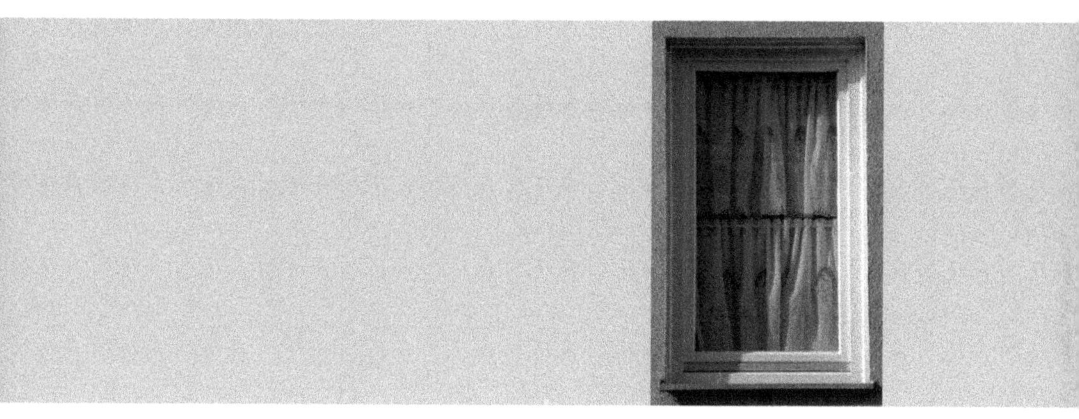

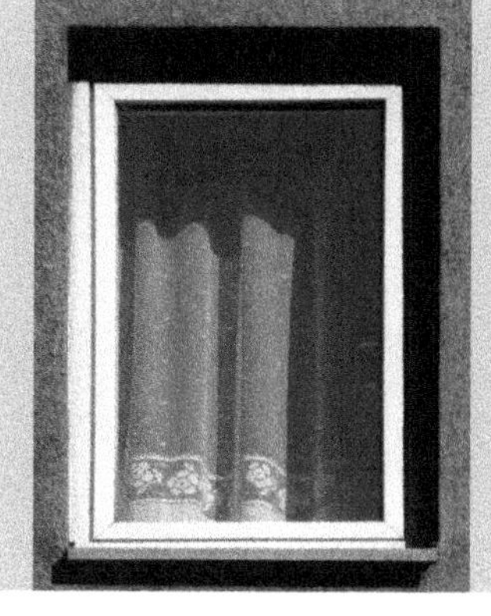

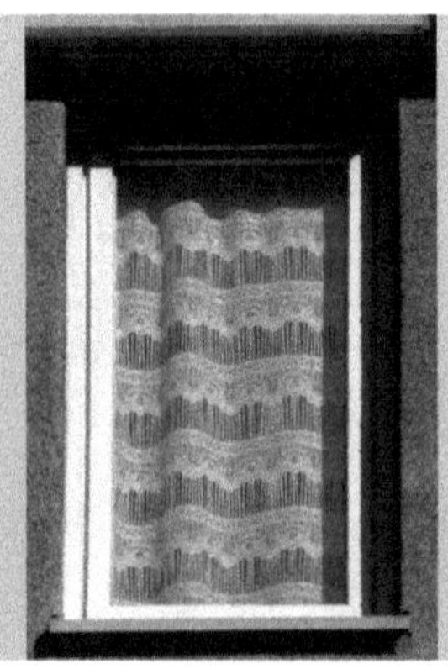

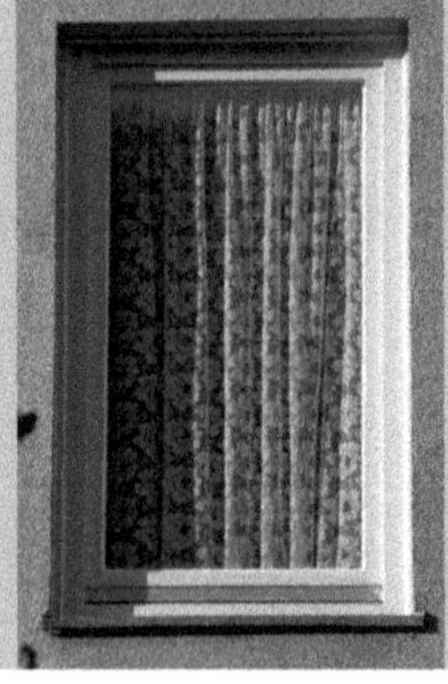

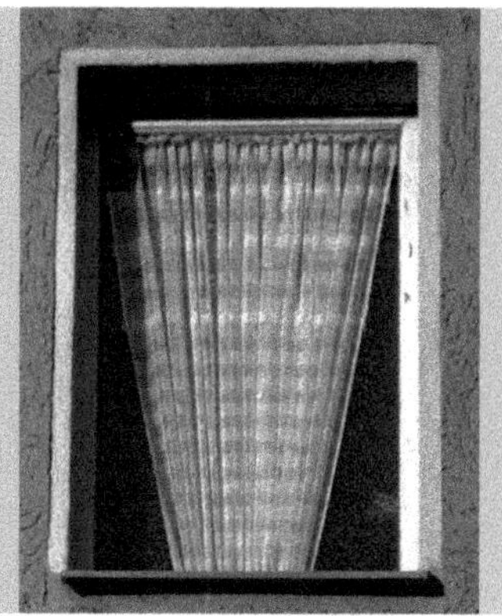

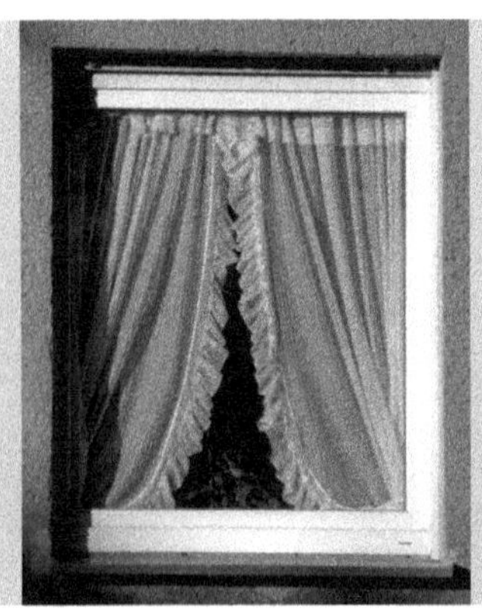

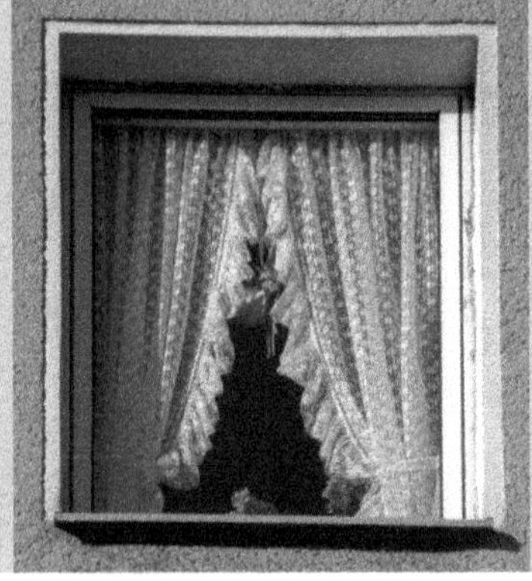

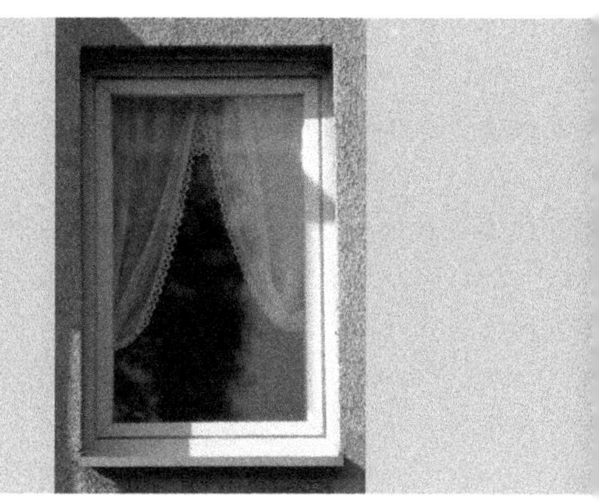

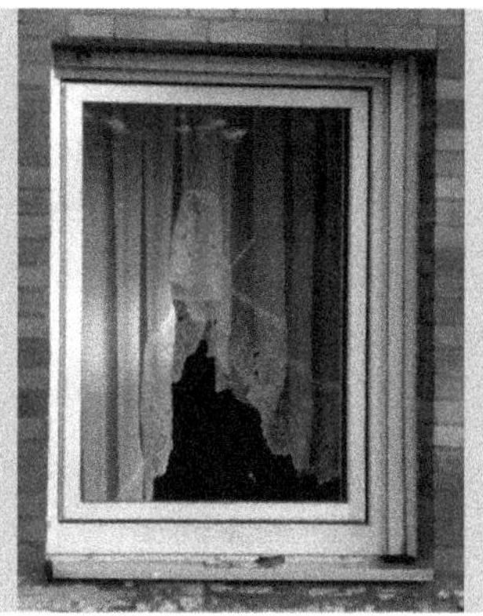

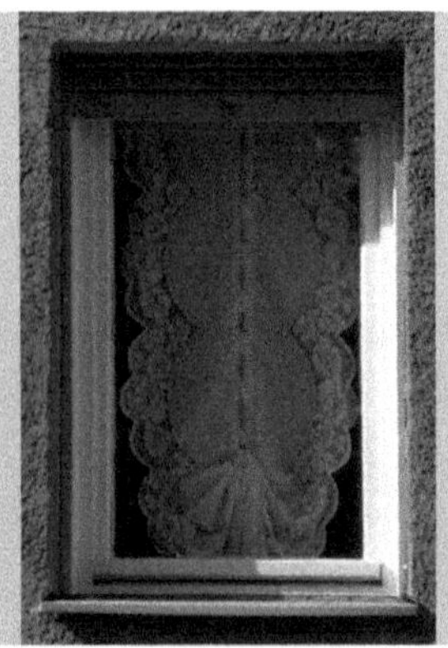

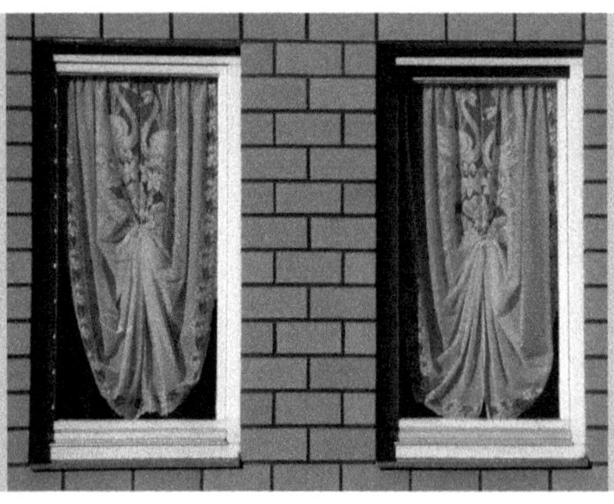

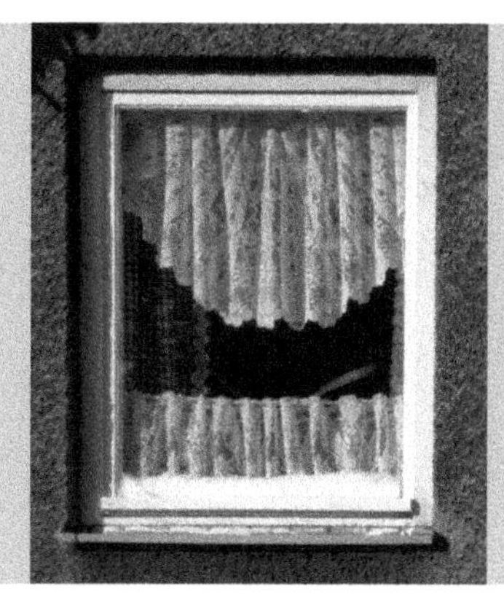

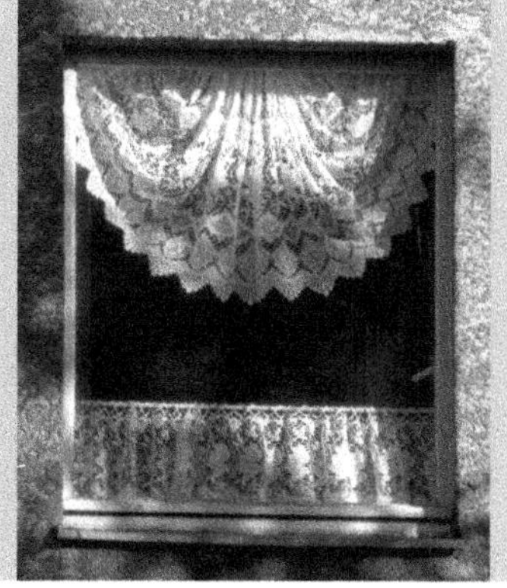

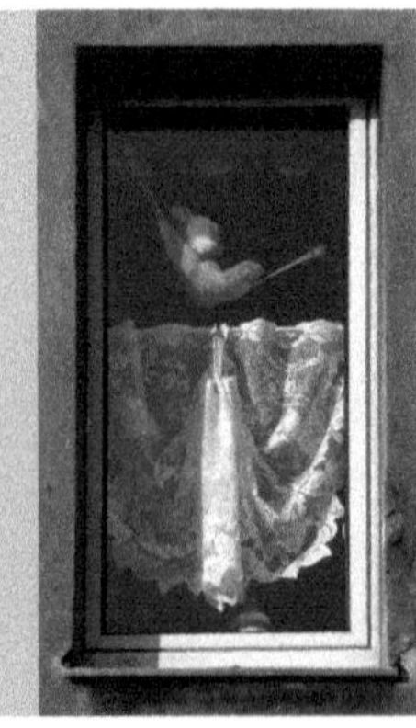

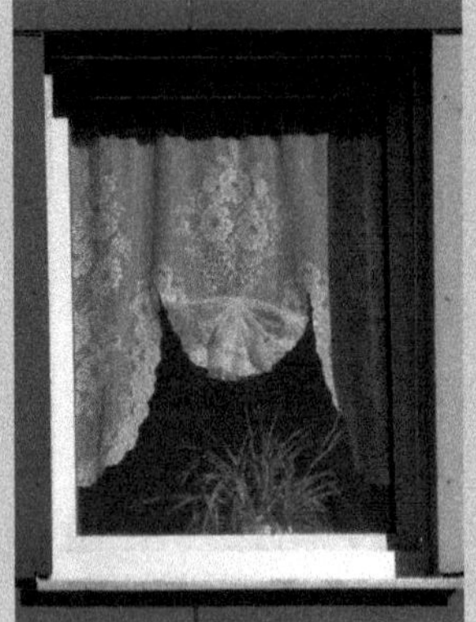

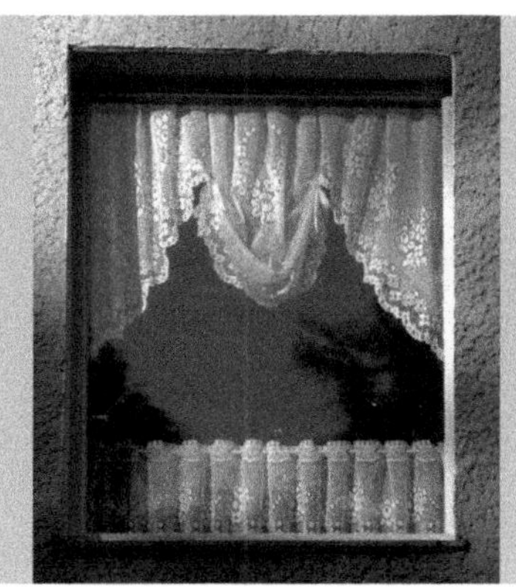

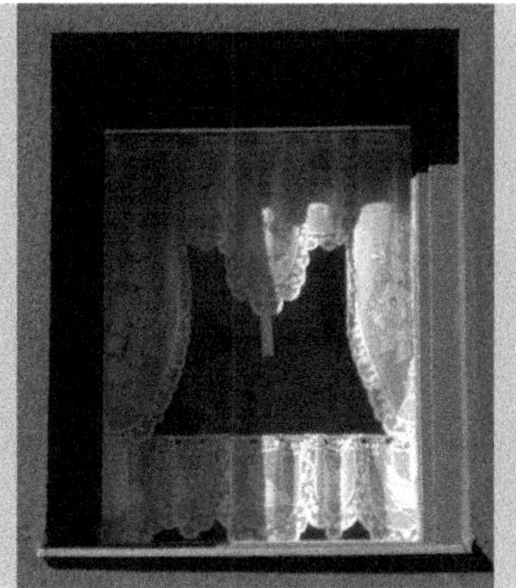

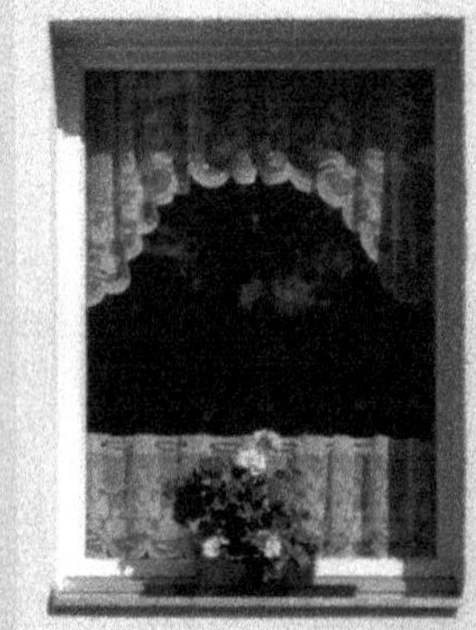

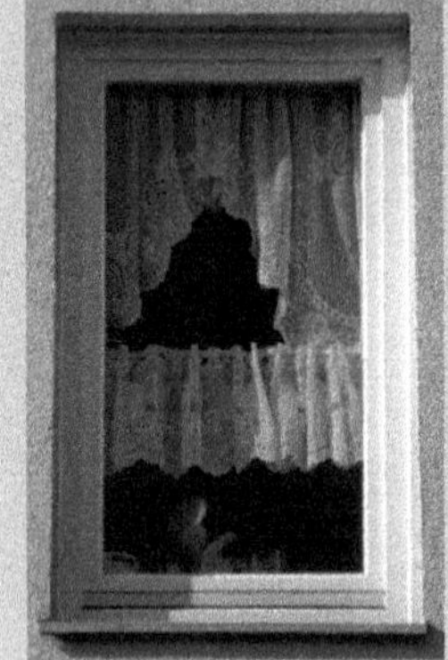

FORSTER STREET COLLECTION

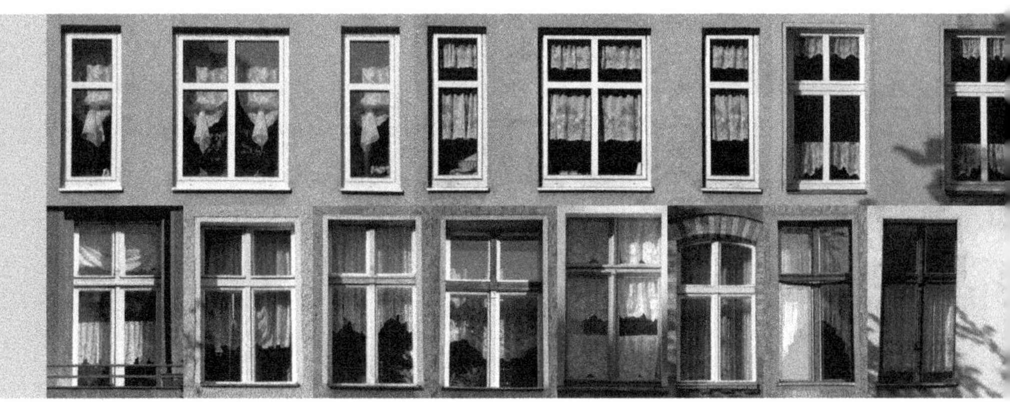

30 pictures

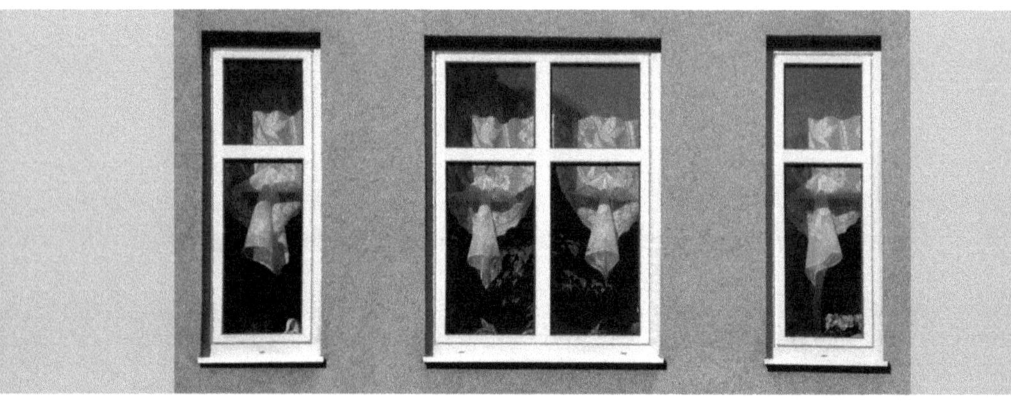

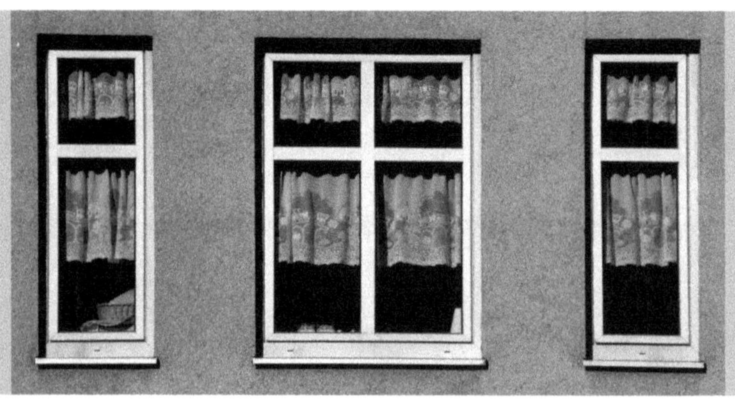

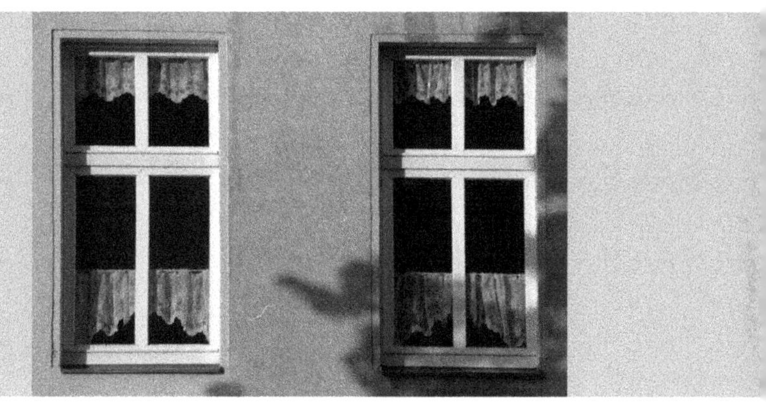

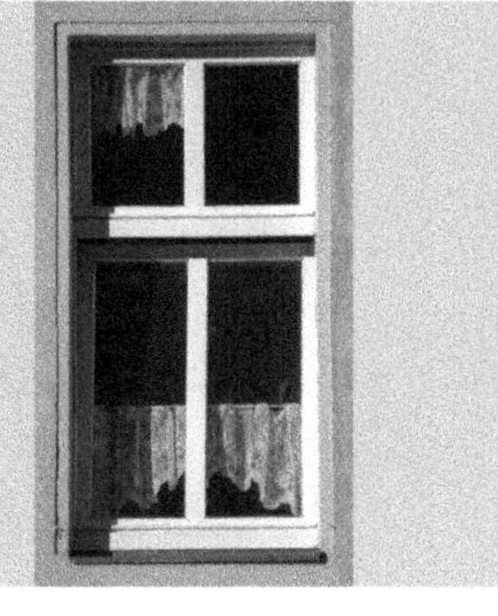

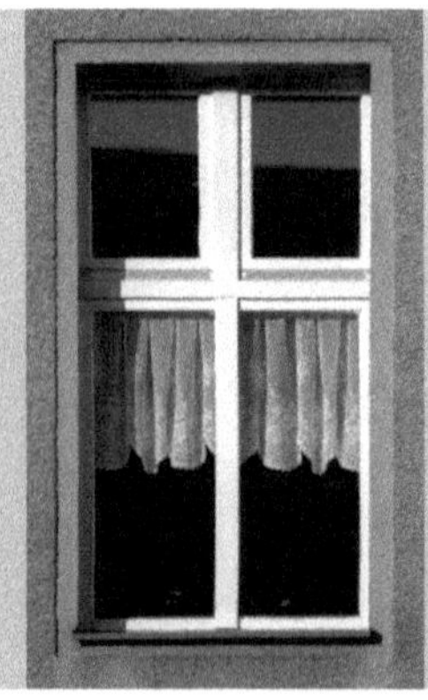

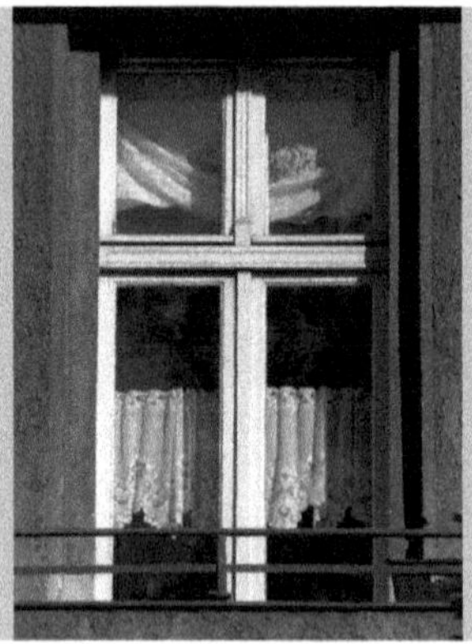

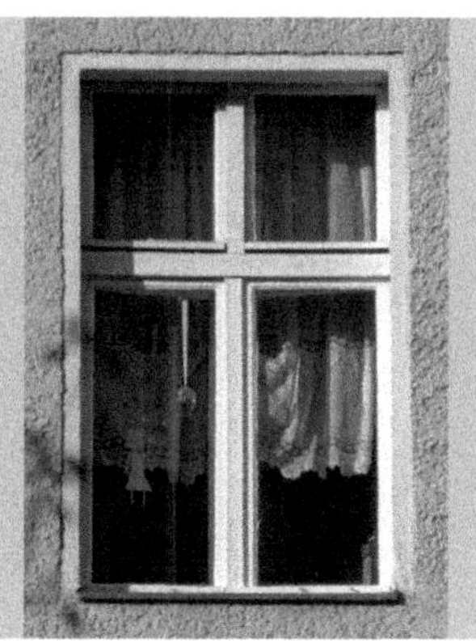

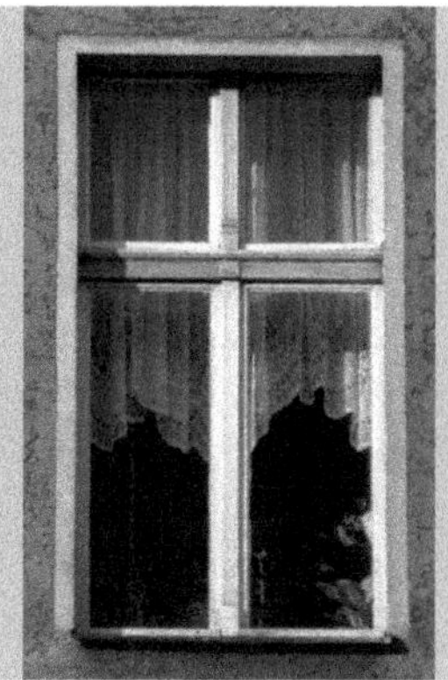

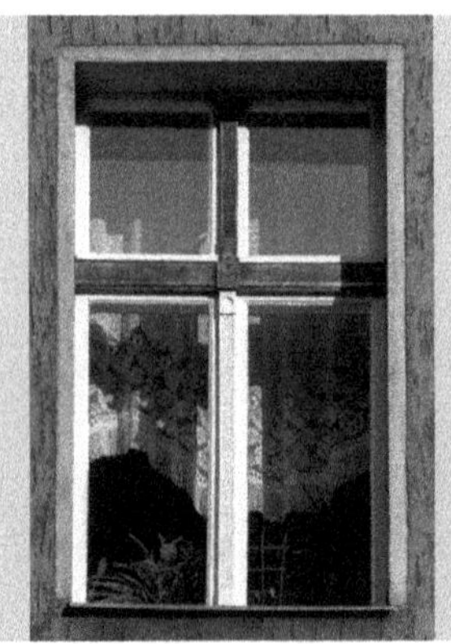

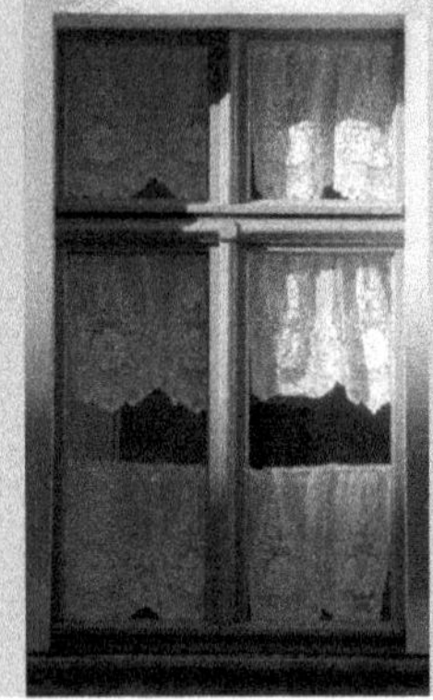

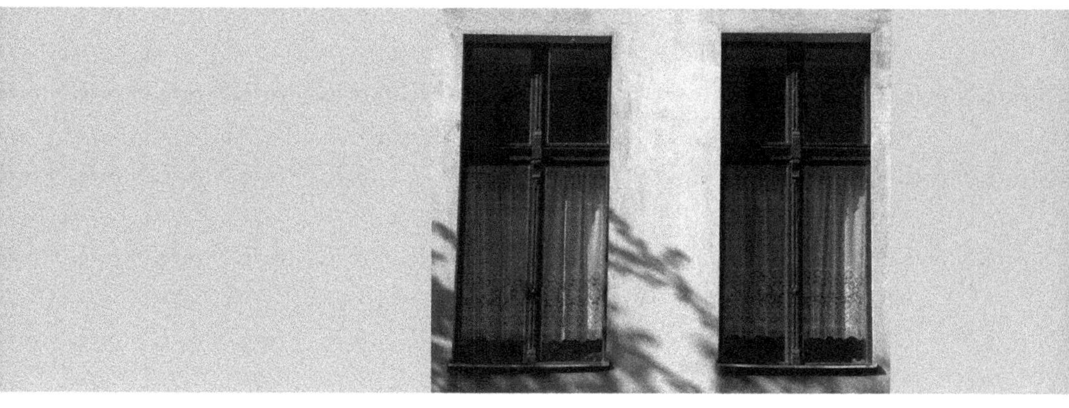

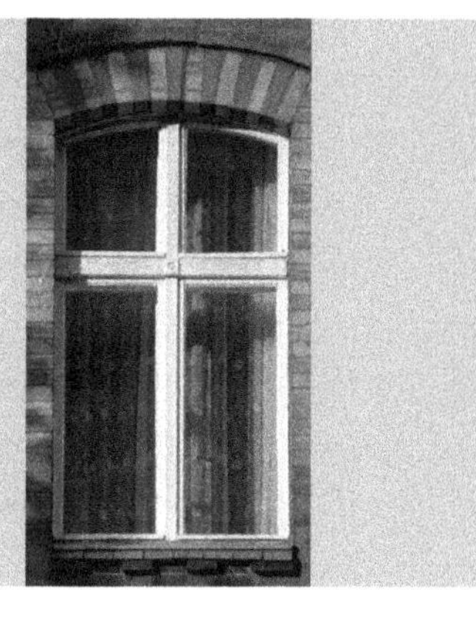

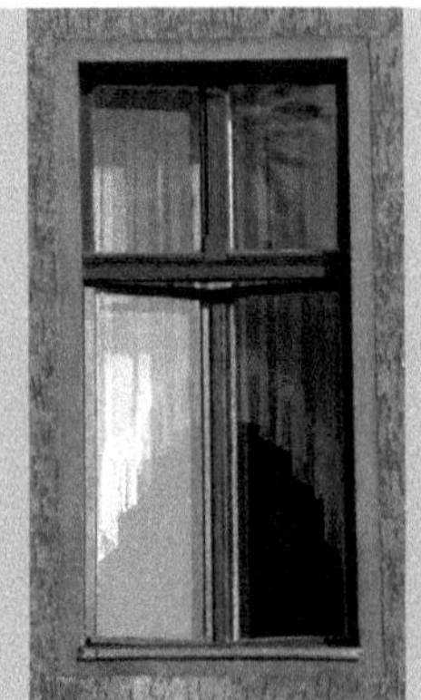

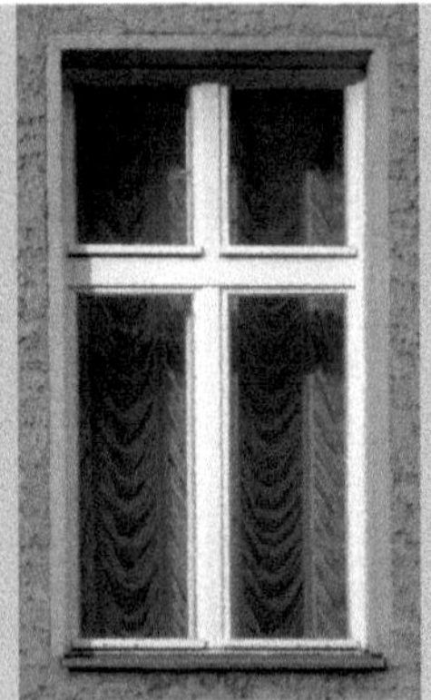

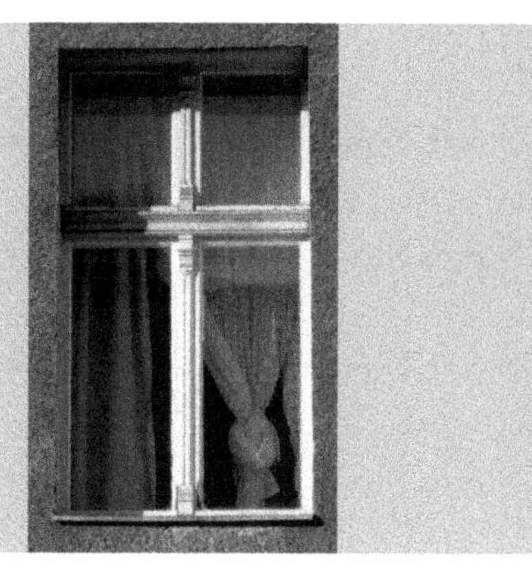

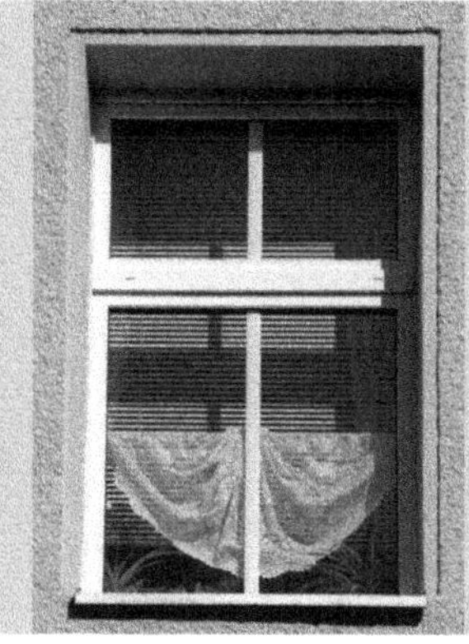

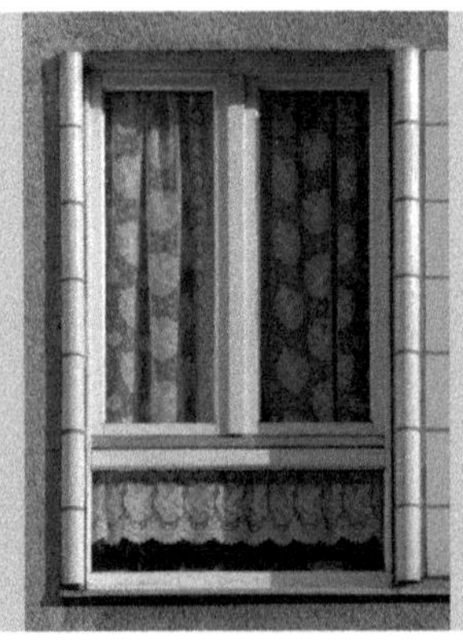

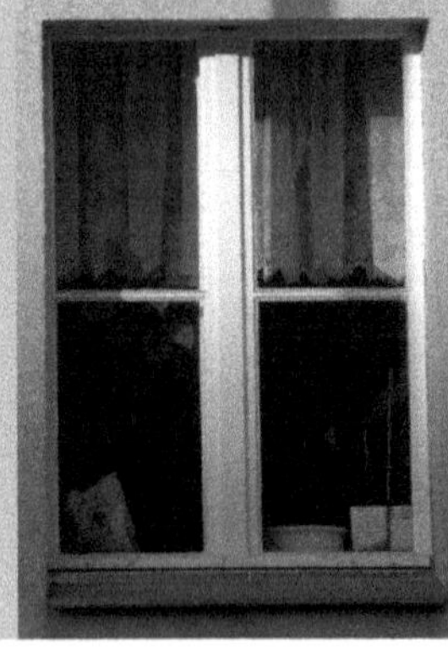

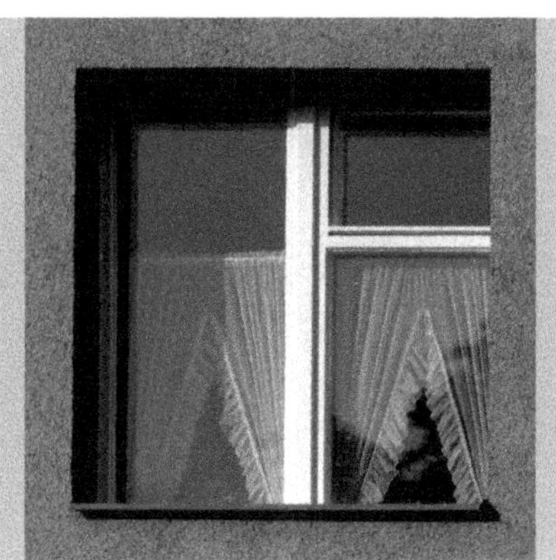

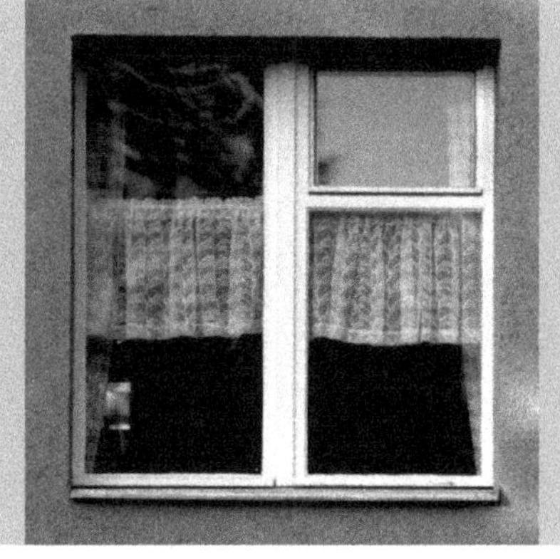

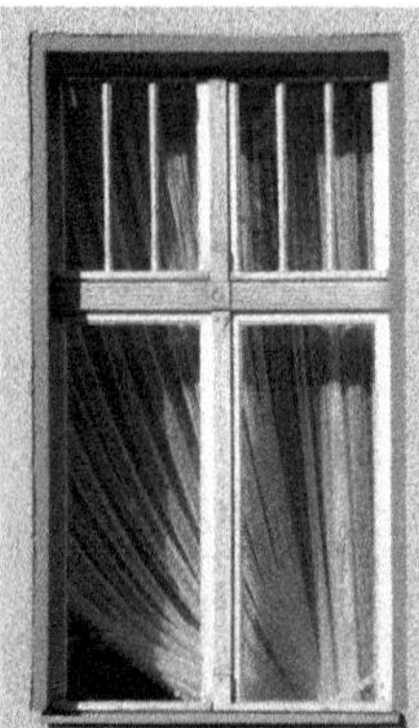

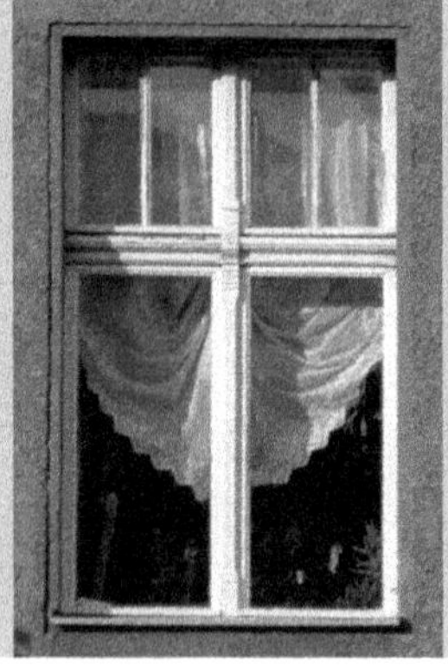

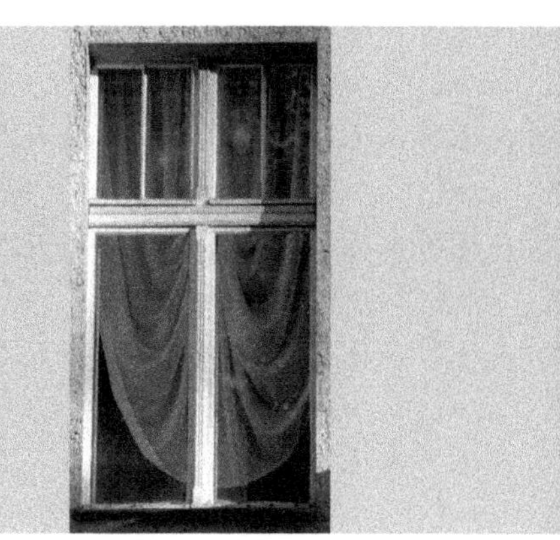

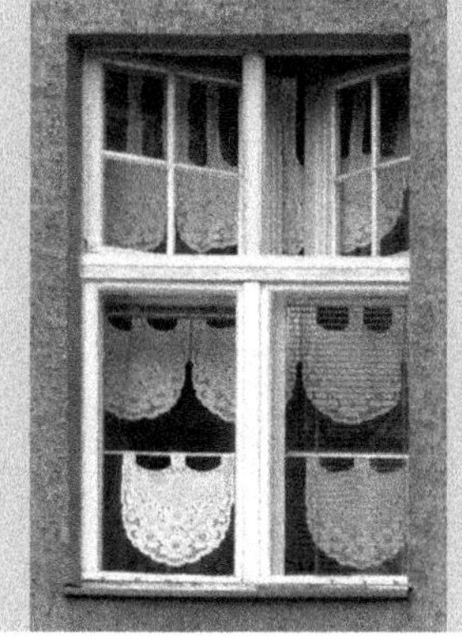

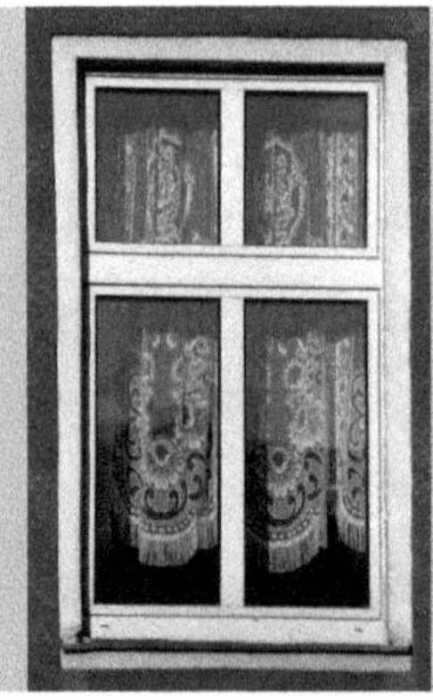

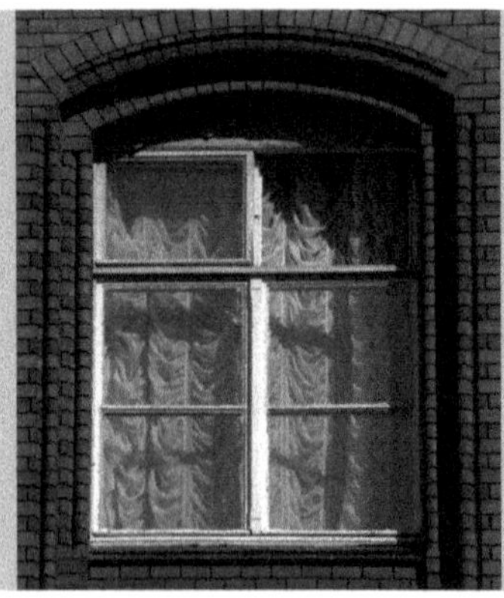

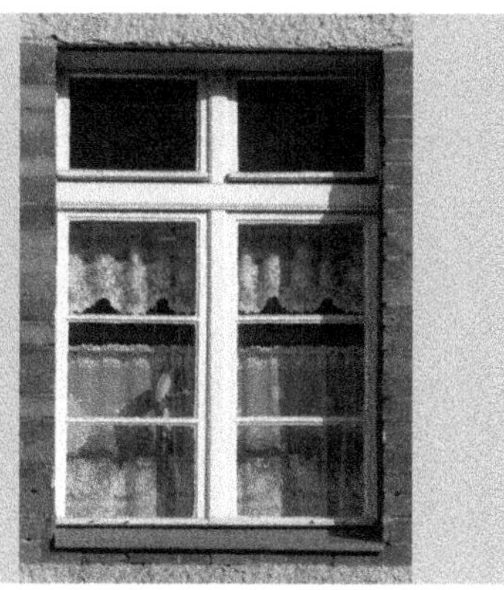

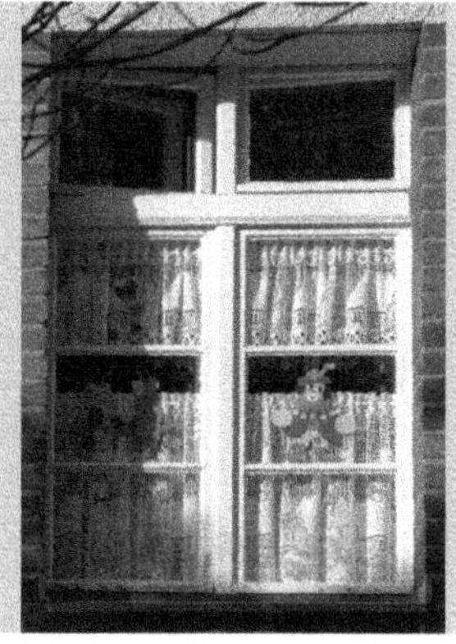

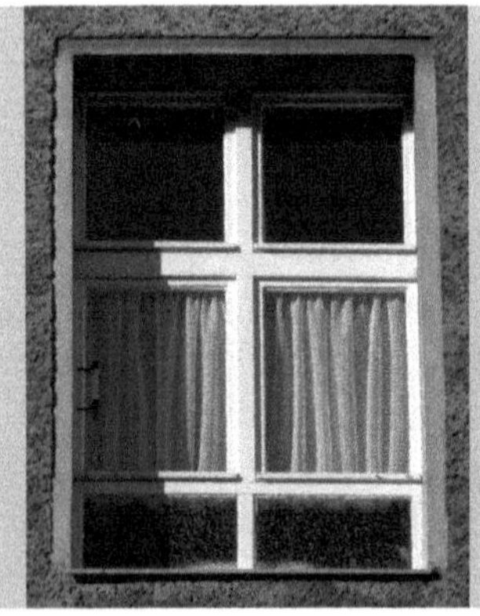

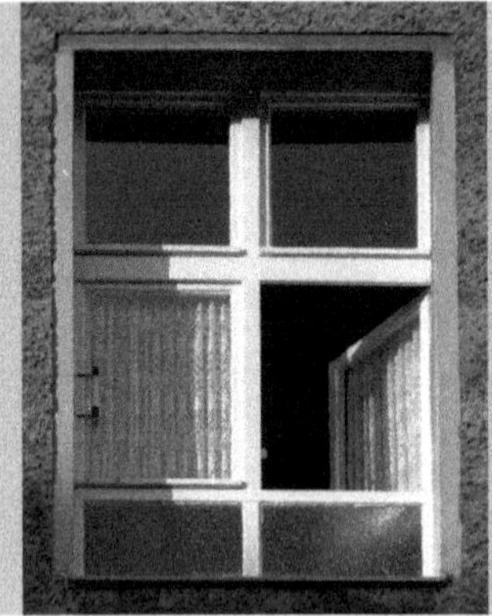

GÖRLITZER STREET COLLECTION

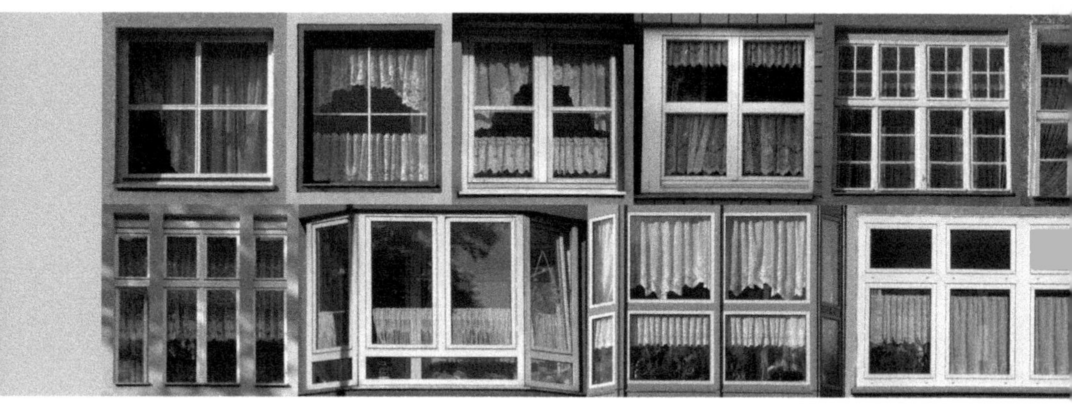

12 pictures

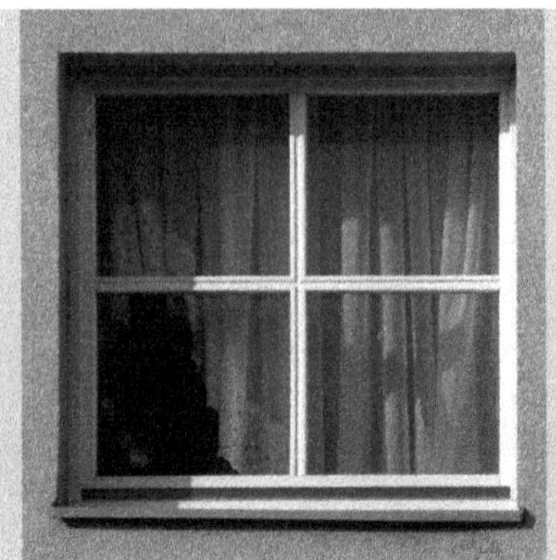

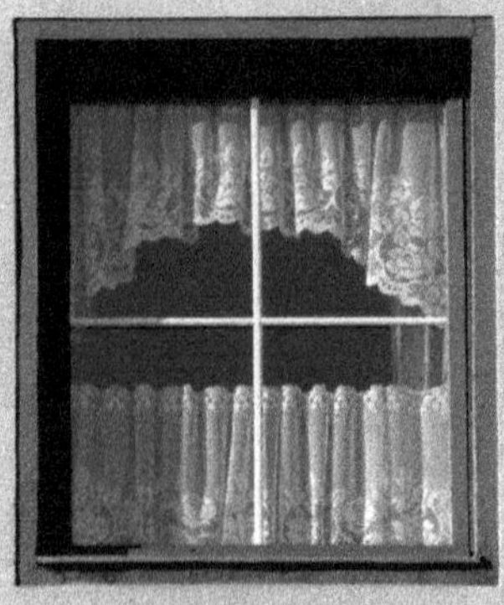

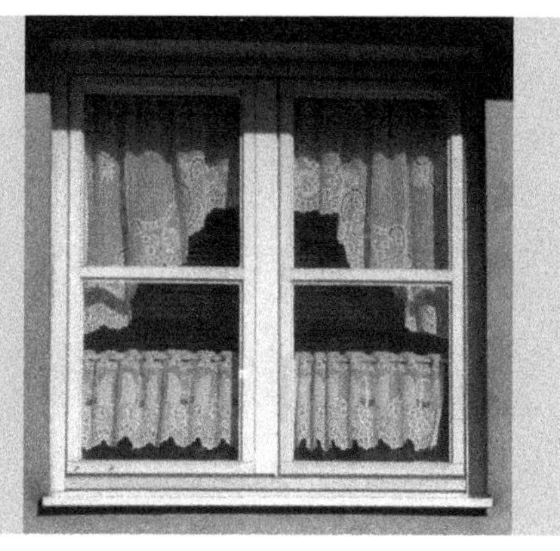

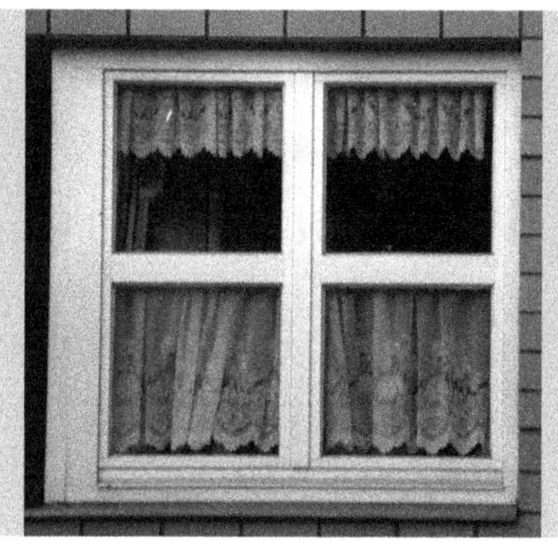

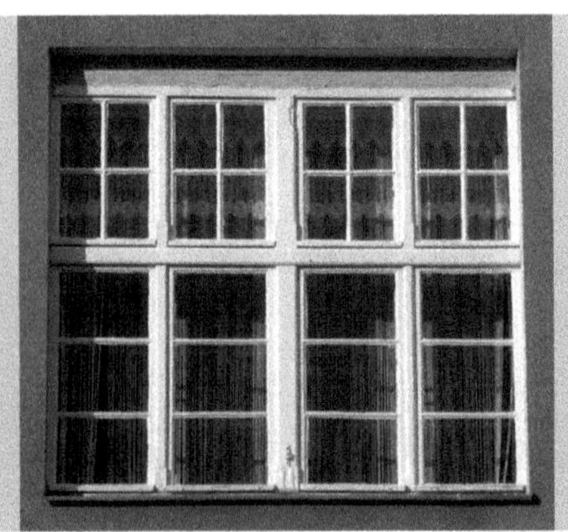

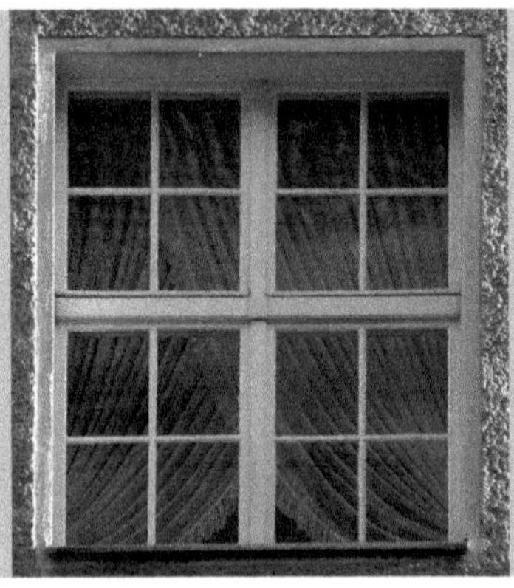

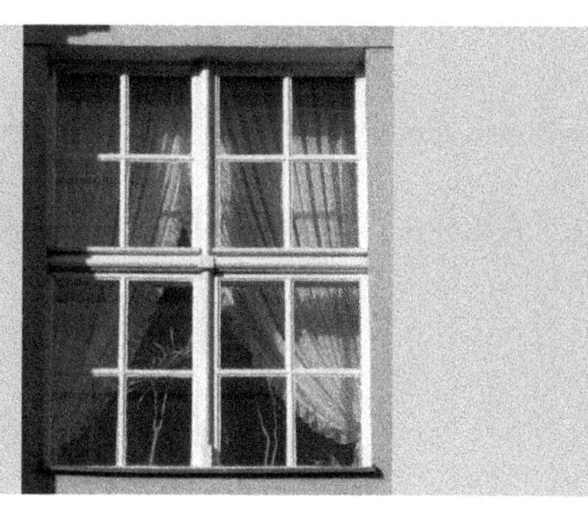

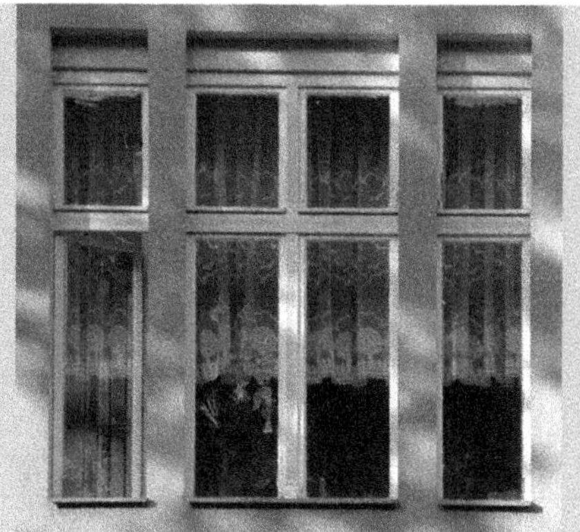

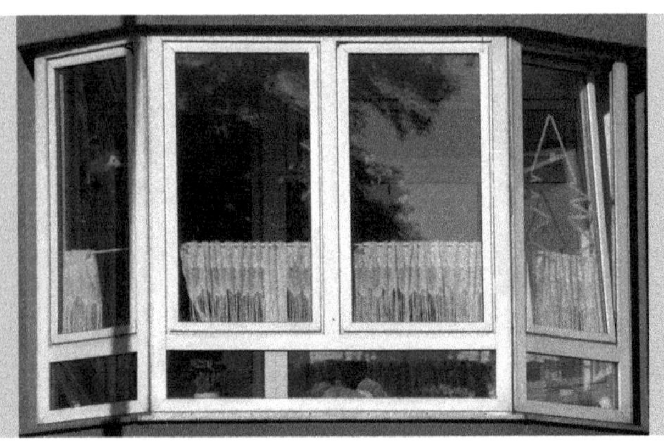

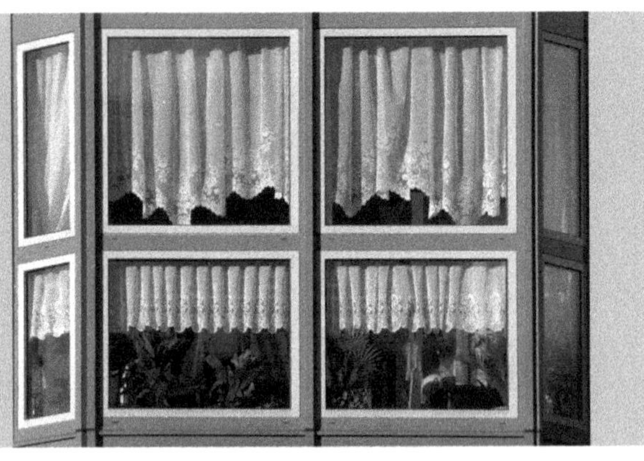

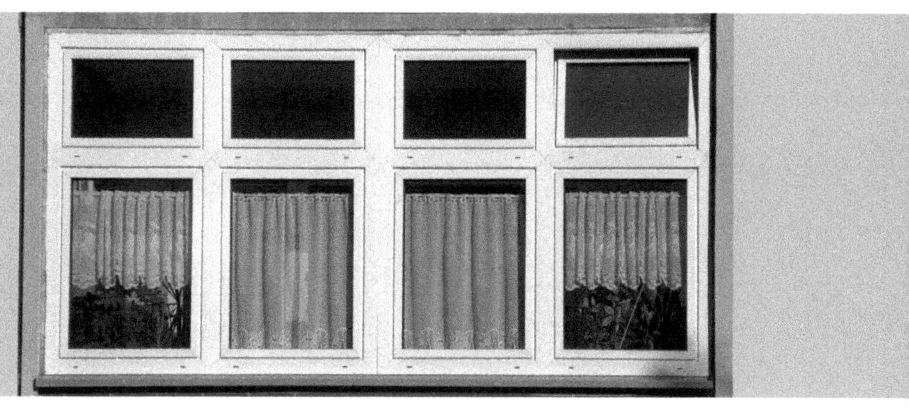

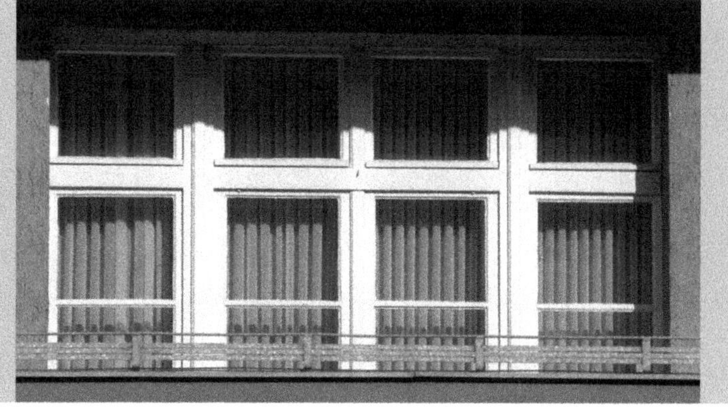

LIEGNITZER STREET COLLECTION

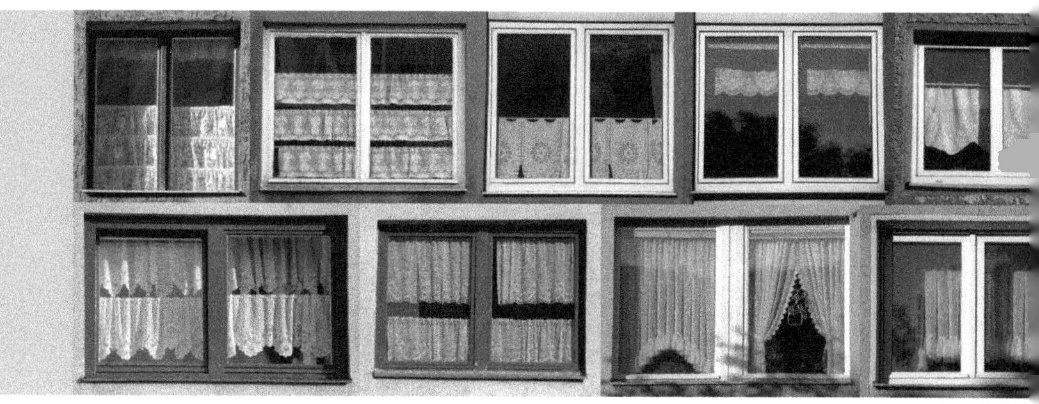

26 pictures

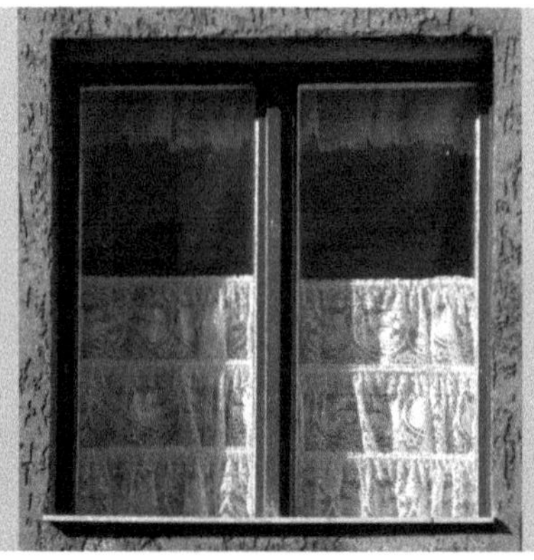

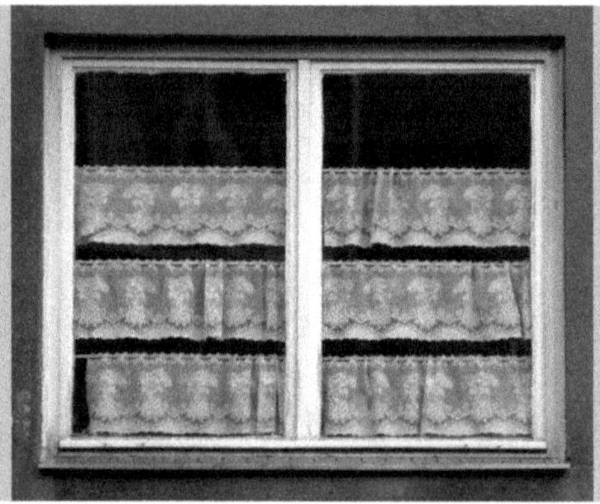

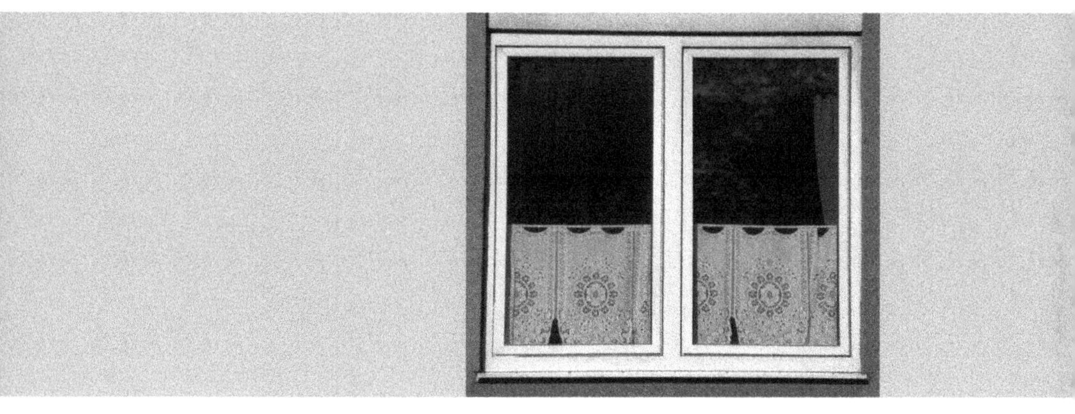

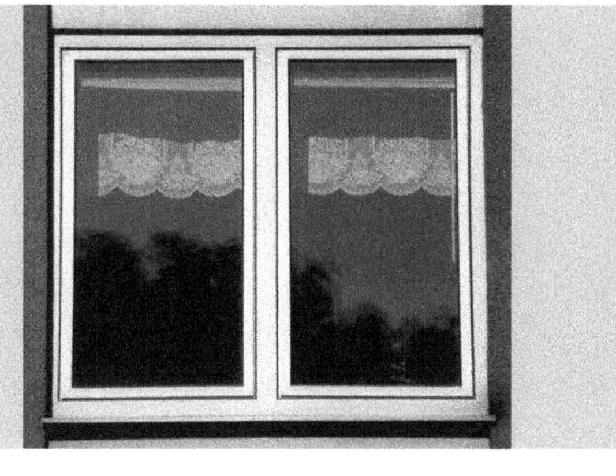

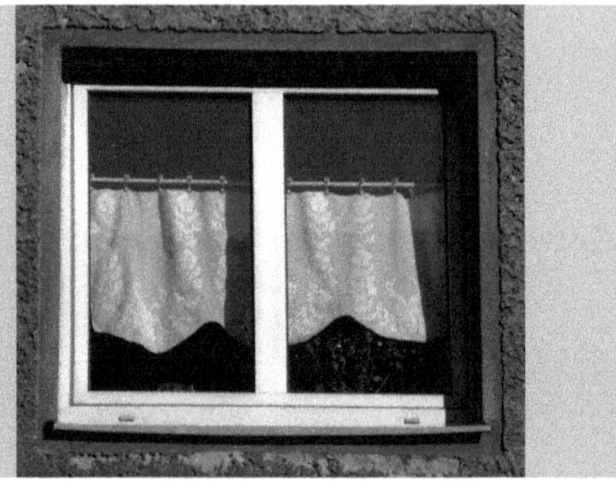

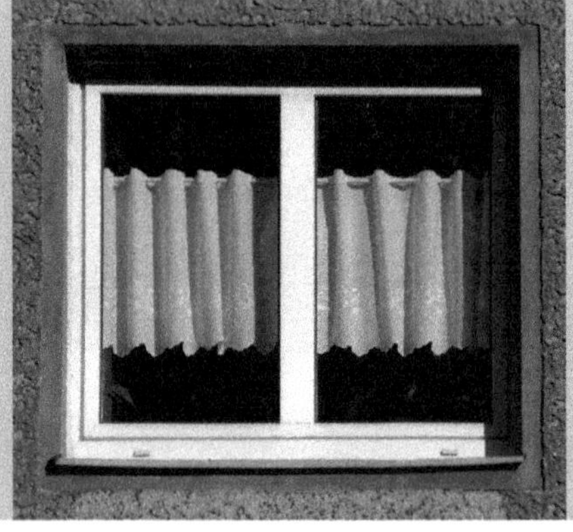

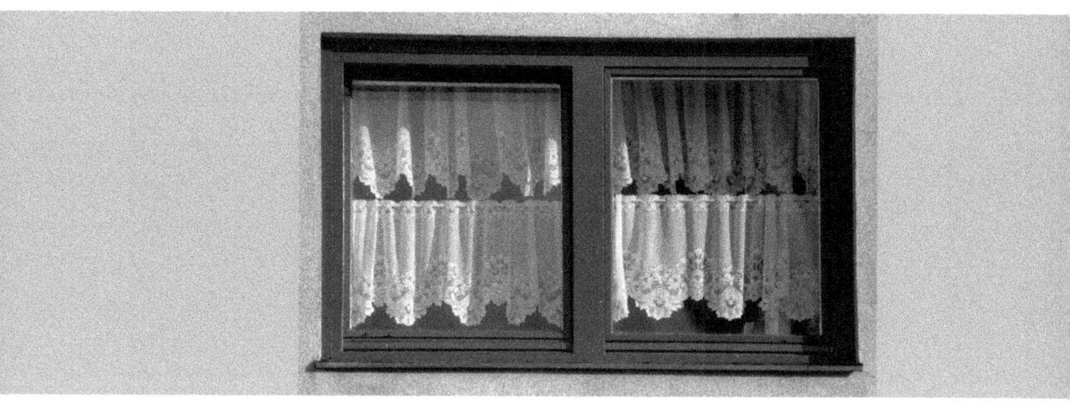

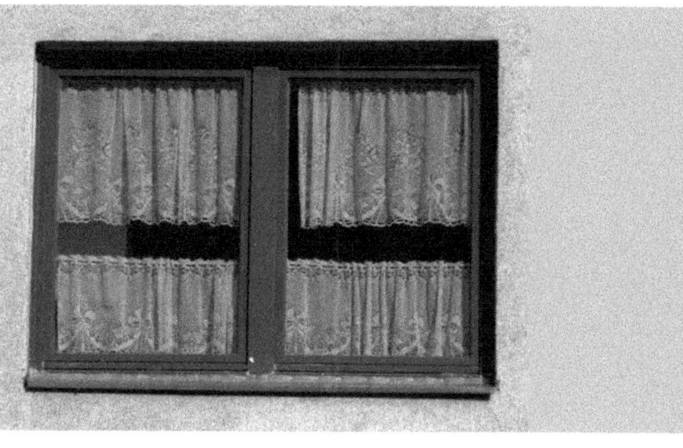

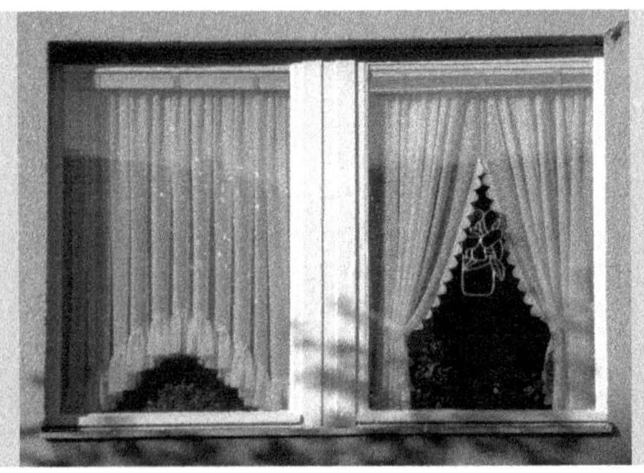

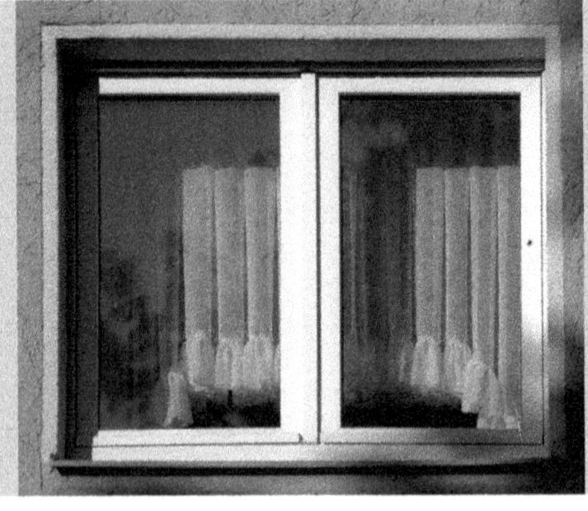

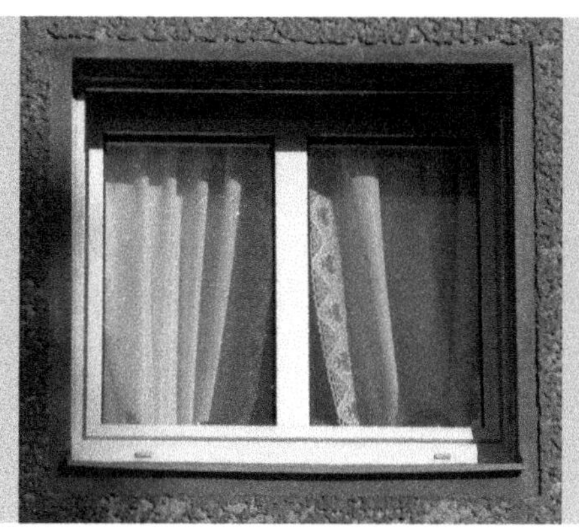

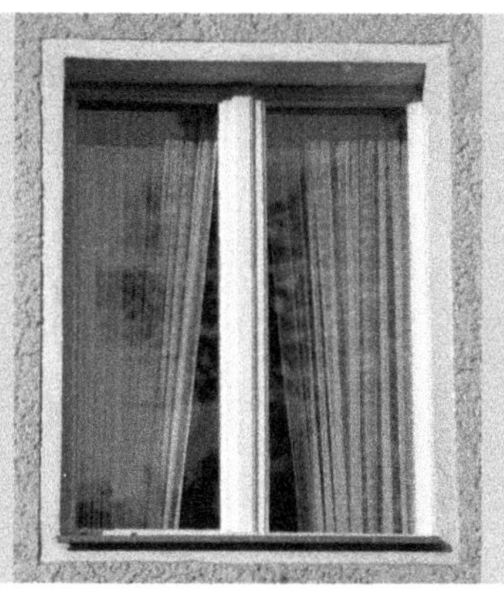

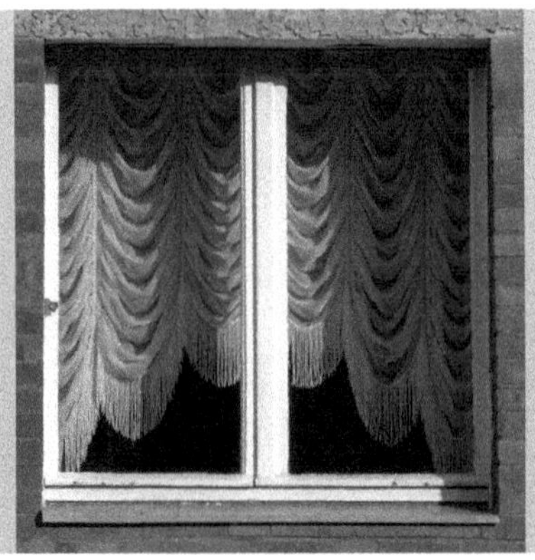

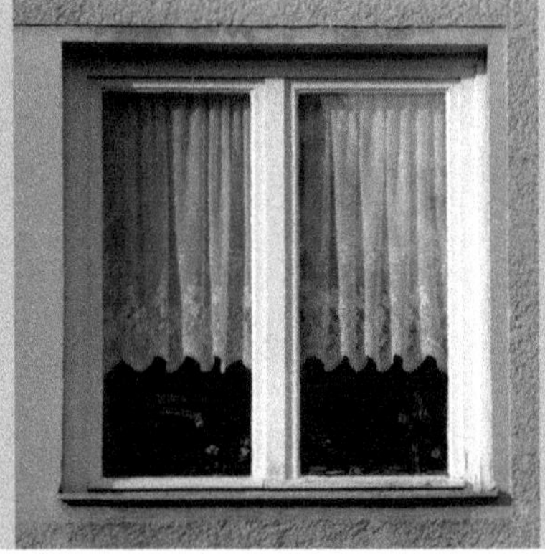

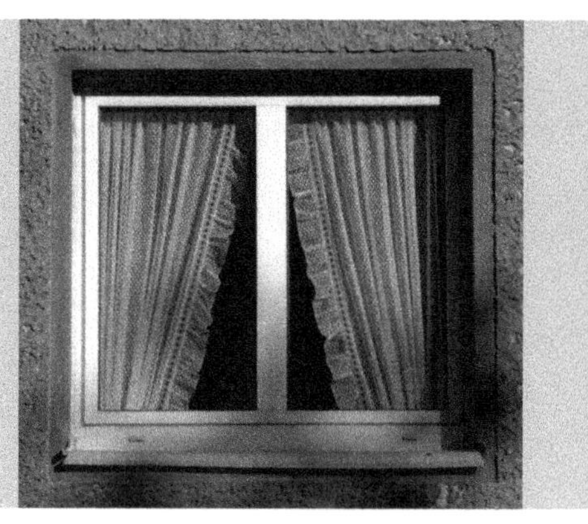

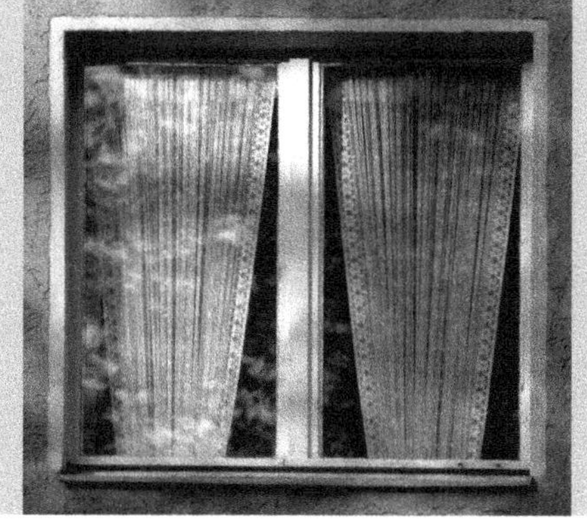

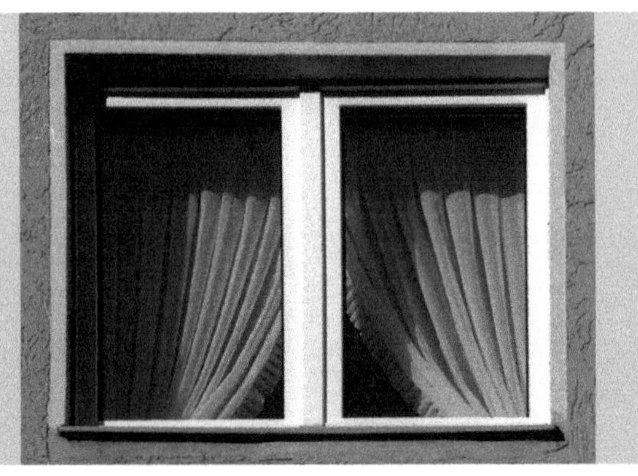

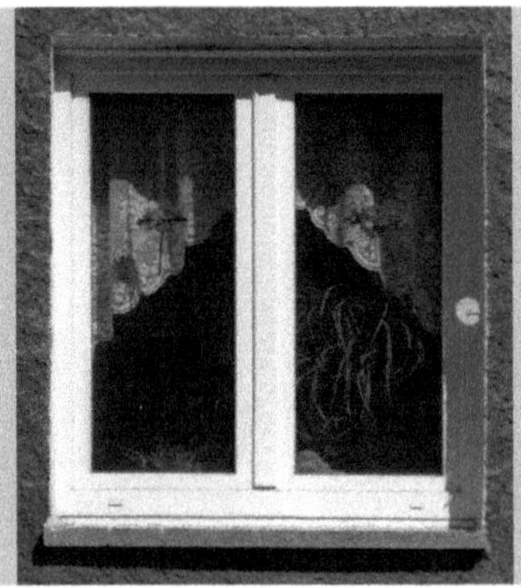

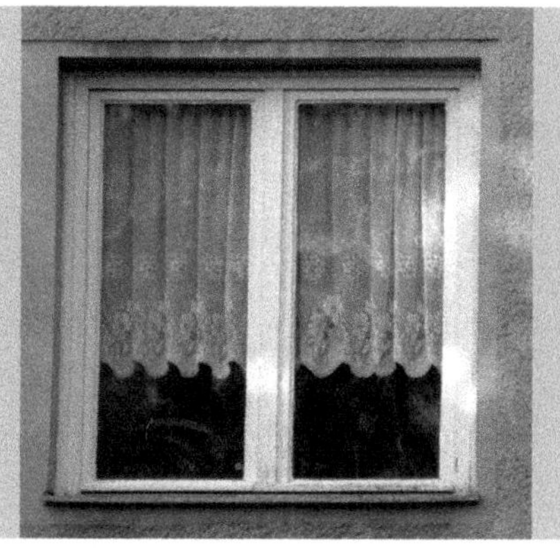

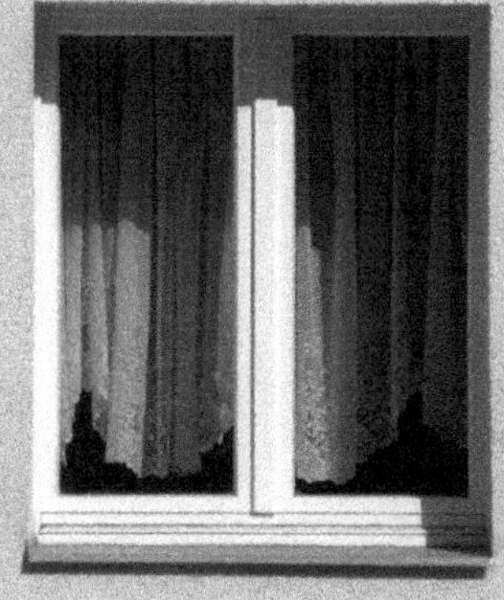

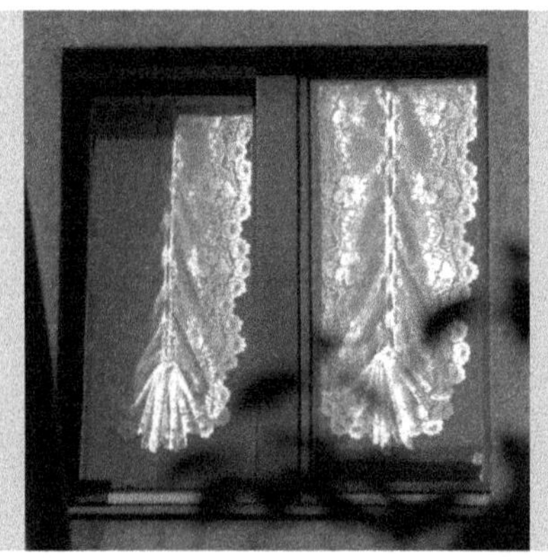

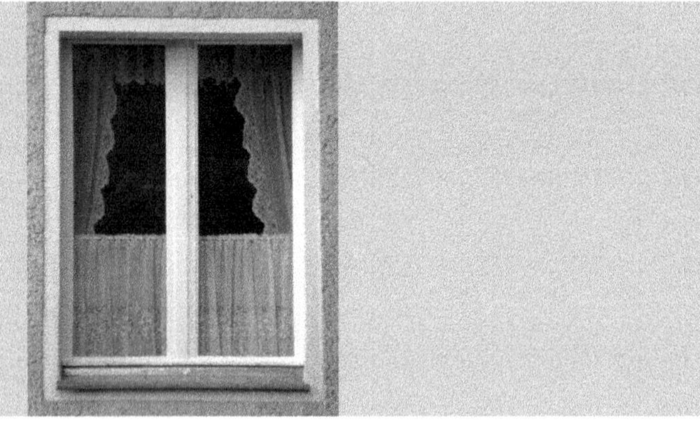

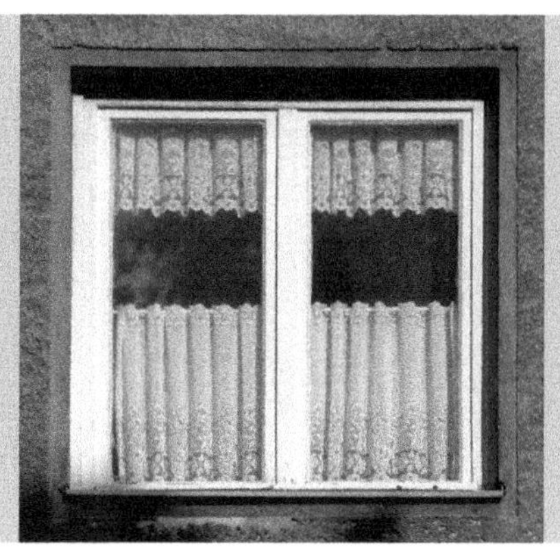

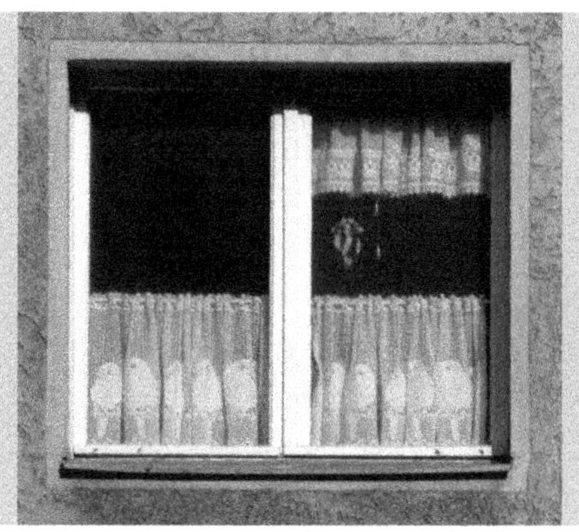

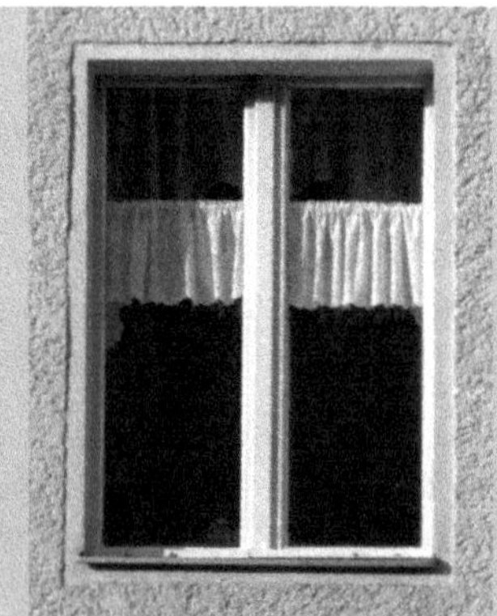

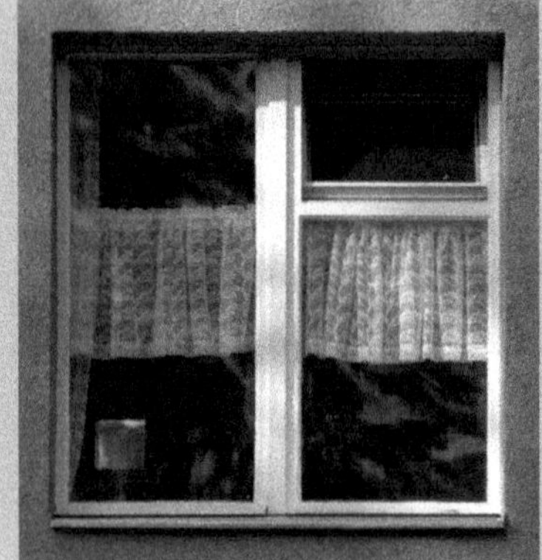

REICHENBERGER STREET COLLECTION

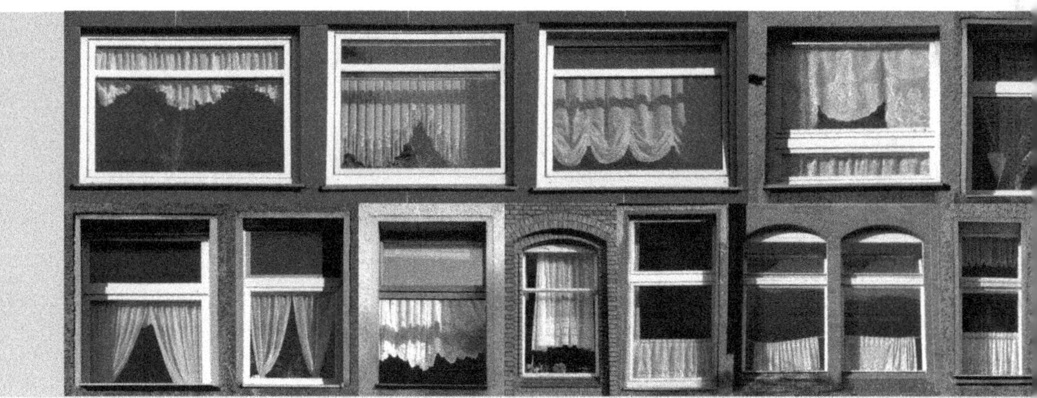

14 pictures

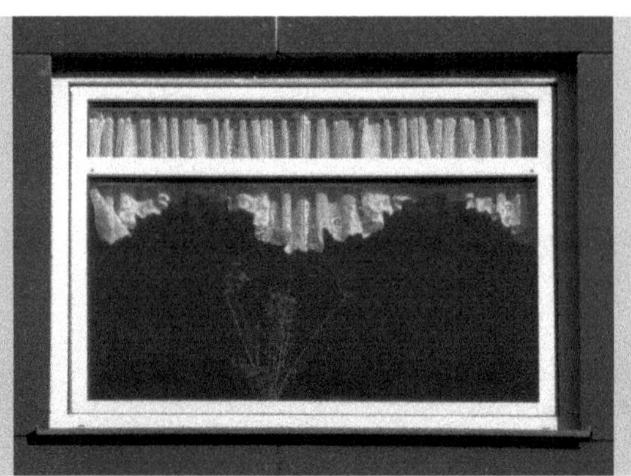

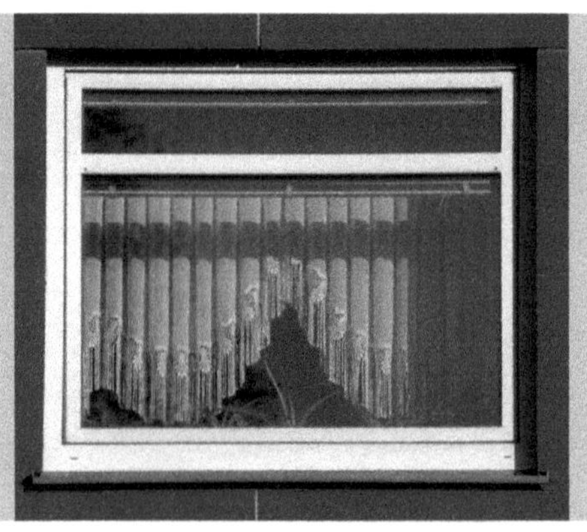

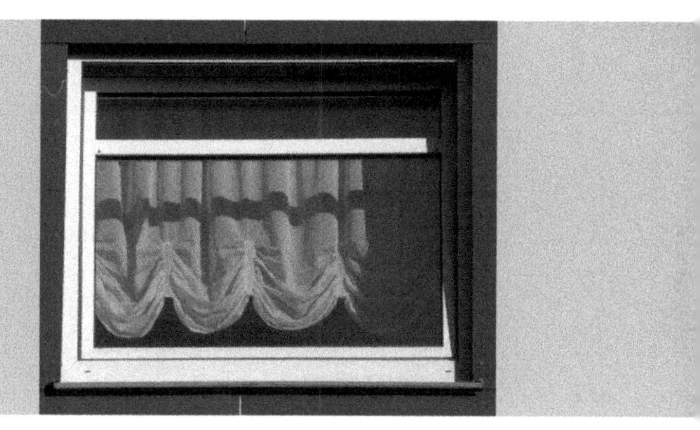

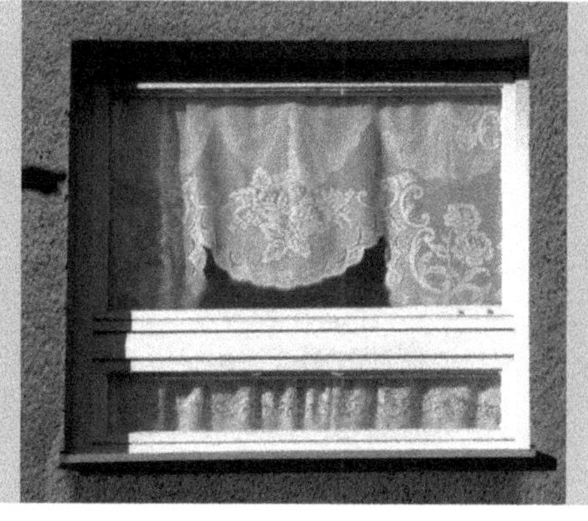

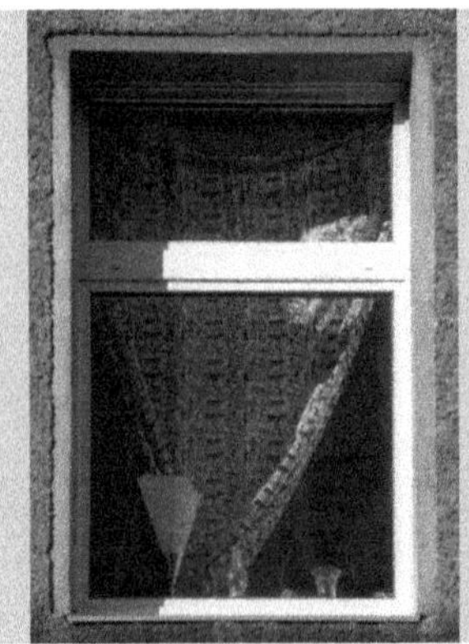

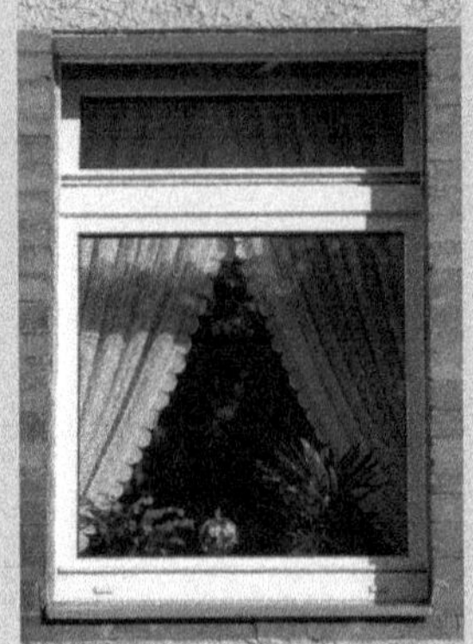

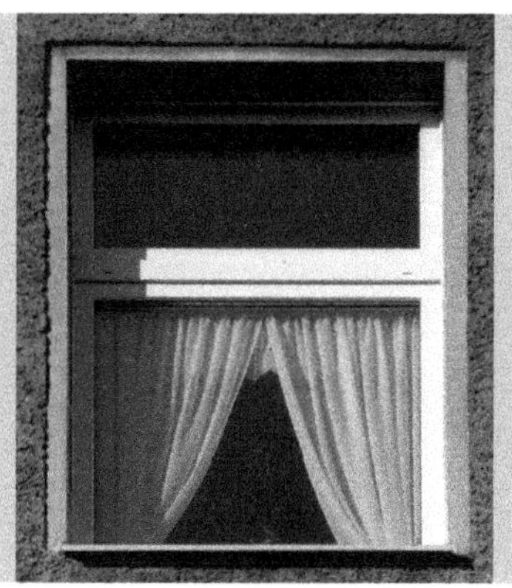

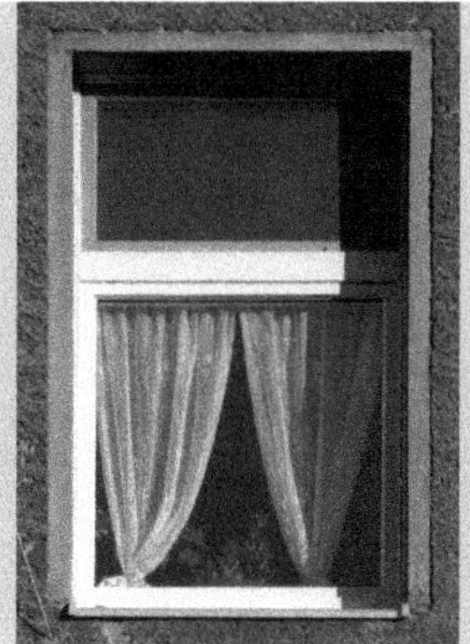

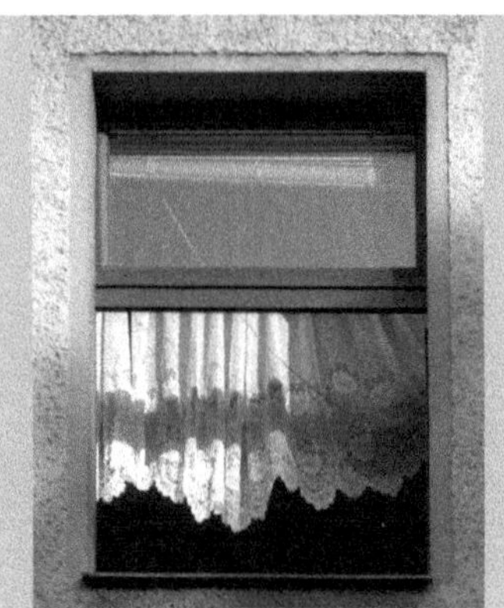

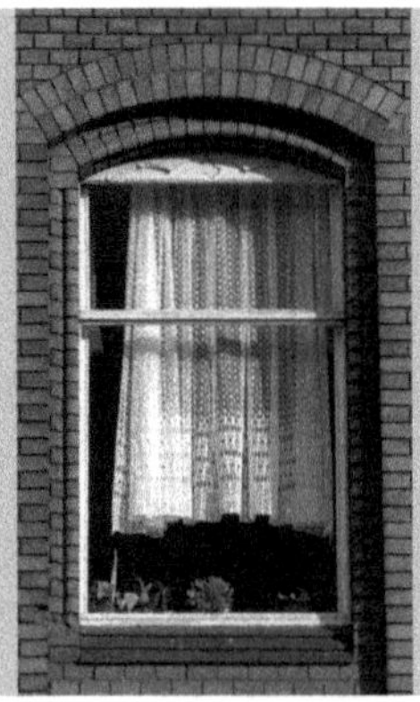

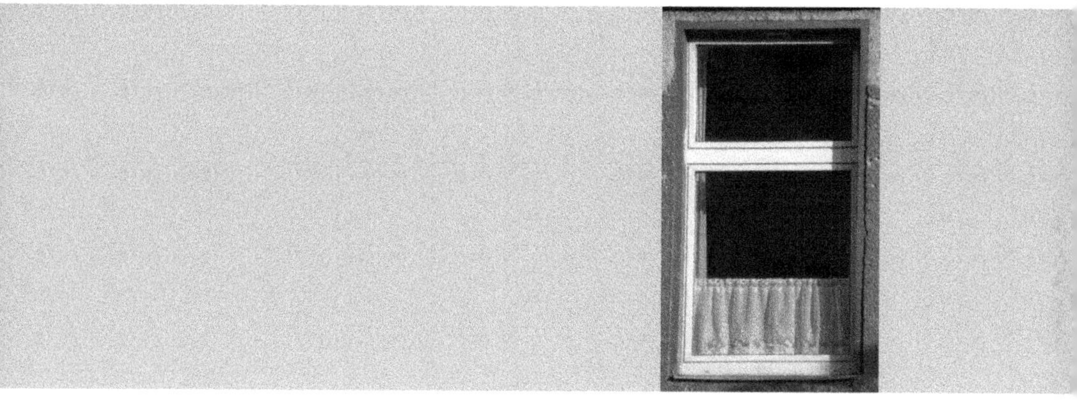

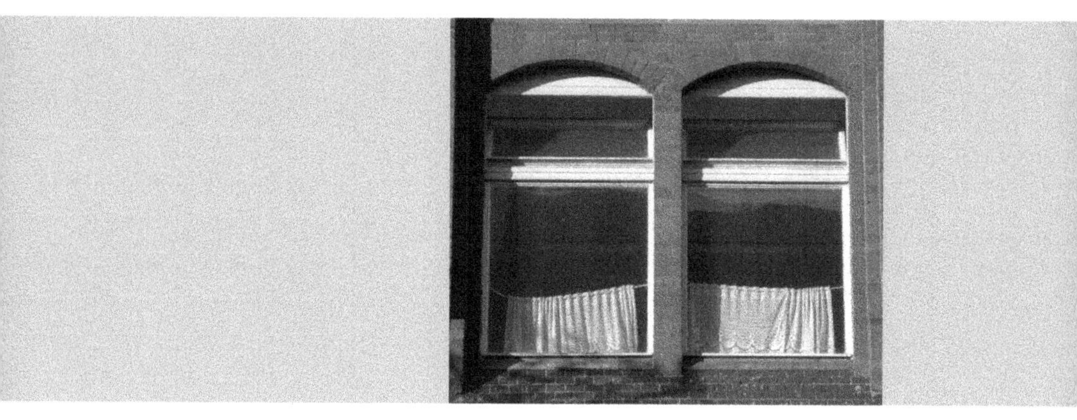

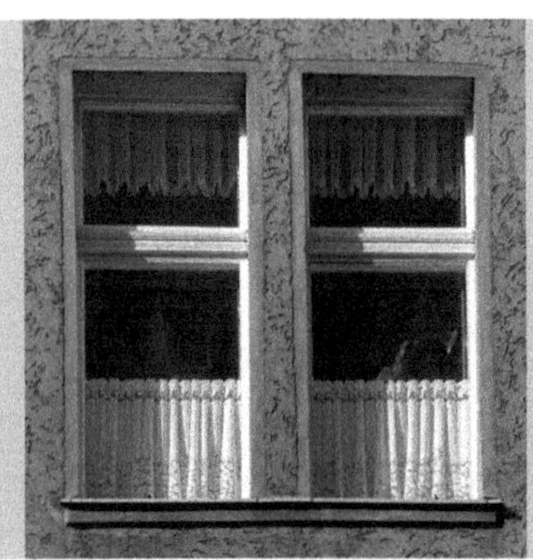

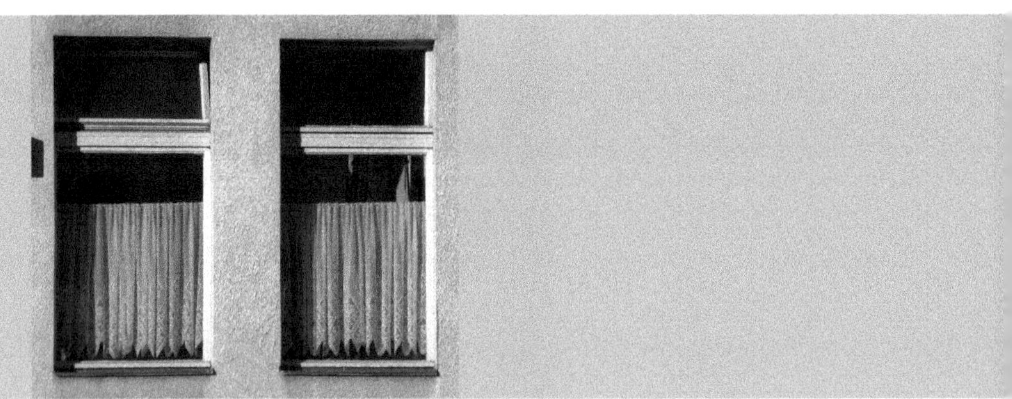